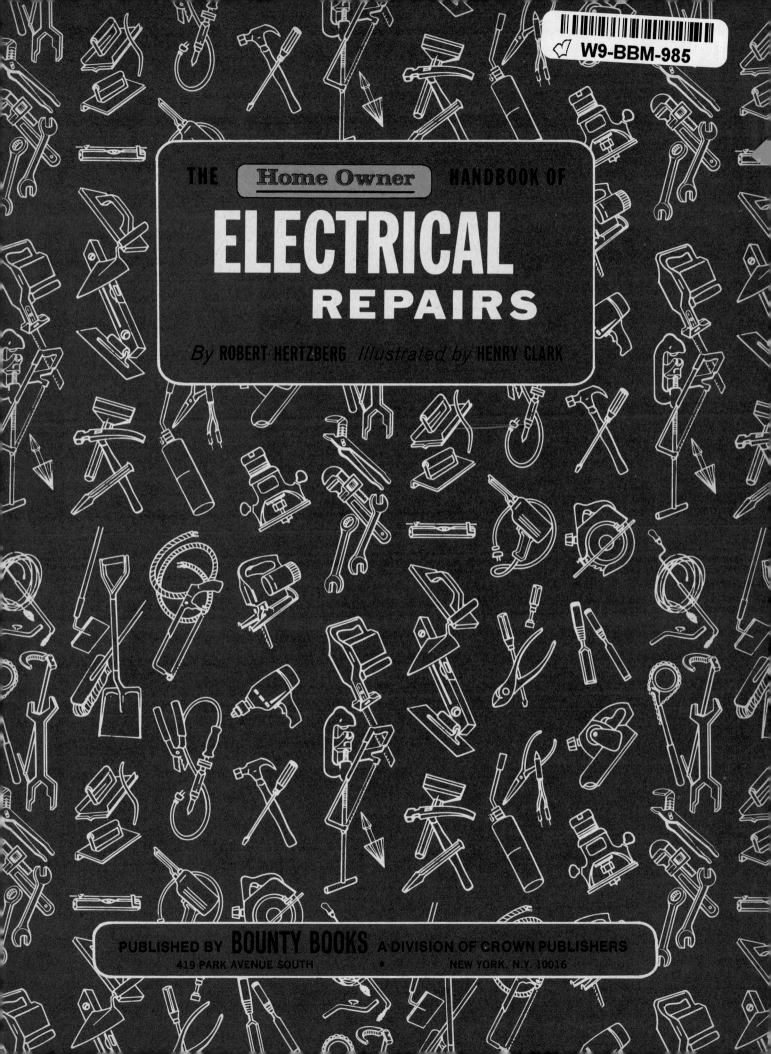

THE Home Owner HANDBOOK OF
ELECTRICAL REPAIRS

By ROBERT HERTZBERG   *Illustrated by* HENRY CLARK

PUBLISHED BY **BOUNTY BOOKS** A DIVISION OF CROWN PUBLISHERS
419 PARK AVENUE SOUTH   •   NEW YORK, N.Y. 10016

W9-BBM-985

LARRY EISINGER: *President/Editor-in-Chief*

ROBERT BRIGHTMAN: *Editor* • JACQUELINE BARNES: *Associate Editor*

L. E. MARSH: *Art Director* • JOHN CERVASIO: *Art Editor*

HOWARD KATZ: *Production*

Special Photography by FRED REGAN

ACKNOWLEDGMENTS

We gratefully acknowledge the help of the following firms:

General Electric Company
Sylvania
Heathkit Company
Long Island Lighting
Nutone, Inc.
Scovill Corporation
Thomas Industries, Inc.
Westinghouse Corporation

Allied Radio
Amana Corporation
Bryant Electric
Carrier Corporation
Consolidated Edison
East Coast Lighting
Frigidaire Corporation

Created by EISINGER PUBLICATIONS, Inc.
233 Spring Street, New York, N.Y. 10013

CONTENTS

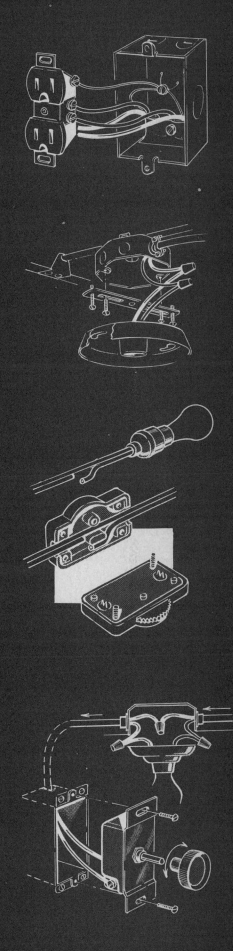

Tall smoke stacks are the sign of a big electric generating station. Because of the huge amounts of fuel necessary to operate the boilers, most such plants are located at a water site or railroad siding.

Basic Facts About Electricity

Even if you do not make any elaborate electric repairs, you should know all about WATTS, AMPERES AND VOLTS.

YOU DON'T HAVE TO KNOW a thing about electricity to enjoy the conveniences of electrical appliances—press the switches and the power company does the rest. However, you're bound to feel annoyed—and angry with your own helplessness—the first time your air conditioner conks out, or your water heater produces only cold water, or your coffee percolator refuses to perk. This is when even a little knowledge might enable you to do something about the situation.

THE POWER HOUSE

Let's start your education where the "juice" starts, in the power station of the local utility company. Here, huge rotating machines generate current that changes its direction periodically. It goes one way for 1/120th of a second, then the other way for another 1/120th, and keeps repeating itself. Each of these movements is called an "alternation;" hence the common term "alternating current," or "AC." Two complete alternations comprise a "cycle," or, to use the newer international term, a "hertz." The number of hertz per second (hz) is called the frequency. In the United States all the current furnished to homes is 60 hz, but for some industrial purposes it can be 25 or 400 hz. In other countries it is most likely to be 50 hz, but odd values such as 40, 42, 45, 76 and 100 are known to be in use.

AC generators are run by engines using a

variety of fuels. In most big stations, a water boiler heated by burning coal or oil makes steam at high pressure. This is directed against the blades of a turbine, which turns at high speed. The turbine itself is coupled to or is part of the alternator proper. So-called "atomic powered" electric plants use the same boiler-turbine-alternator combination just described, but the water is turned to steam by heat from a nuclear reactor instead of from conventional fuel.

Medium-sized stations use automobile-type internal combustion engines of either the diesel or spark-ignition type, fueled by oil or gasoline. Some even use regular jet engines borrowed from the aviation industry.

The really big power stations of the world depend on a fuel that is clean and quiet, doesn't burn at all, and costs virtually nothing—water! From natural falls such as those at Niagara, in New York, and man-made falls at Hoover Dam; in Nevada, the water merely drops by gravity through paddle wheels connected to the alternators, and runs out downstream to irrigate thousands of acres of farm land.

The electricity from commercial stations is not a single current alternating at 60 times a second. Actually, it consists of three identical currents, called "phases," timed so that they don't interfere with each other. Three-phase energy is advantageous for the operation of large motors, from about one horsepower and up. All ordinary household appliances run on single-phase current.

THE ELECTRICAL UNITS

Before we get into the important subject of electric-power delivery to the home, let's talk about volts, amperes, ohms and watts. "Voltage" is the pushing action of electricity in the wires of a circuit or appliance. "Ohmage" is their tendency to resist the pressure. Thin wire has a relatively high resistance; thick wire has lower resistance. "Amperage" is a measure of

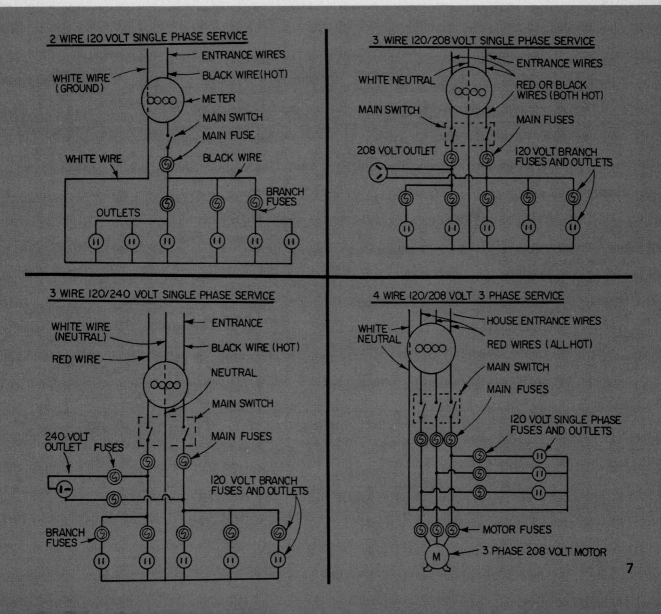

These giant transformers are undergoing installation at a distributing center. Such transformers can handle as much as 175,000 volts. For size comparison, note the truck at the lower left of the photograph.

the electricity pushed through the resistance by the voltage. One ampere is defined as the current that flows for one second through a resistance of one ohm with a pressure of one volt. Note that this is a *rate* of flow, not an amount of current. There is no way of storing electricity for future use, as you can with water from a pipe, because nothing tangible comes out of an electric circuit. What we think of as an electric "current" is a movement of electrons within and between the atoms of the conducting wires. Only when they are in motion do the electrons produce the thermal, magnetic, chemical and various other effects that constitute useful work. When a generator stops turning the electrons return to rest, every appliance or device on the circuit goes dead.

In the technical sense, the term "power" is the *rate* of doing work. The concept of "horsepower," is credited to James Watt, the Scotsman who made the steam engine the greatest labor-saving machine of the 19th Century; one horsepower is the force required to raise 33,000 pounds at the speed of one foot a minute. The electrical power unit is the "watt,"

equal to volts multiplied by amperes. This basic formula must be modified under certain conditions, but suffices for present purposes of explanation.

Since the ampere by itself is a rate, the watt is more correctly the "watt-second." However, the watt-second and two larger units, the watt-minute and the watt-hour, are only very small amounts of electrical work. The more practical unit, for figuring the cost of electric energy, is the "kilowatt-hour," meaning 1,000 watts consumed during 60 minutes. Kilowatt-hours is what the electric meter in your house registers.

HEATING EFFECTS OF ELECTRICITY

In rushing around electric circuits at the speed of light, electrons create heat through mere friction; that is, the energy of their motion is converted to the energy of heat, which in turn can perform valuable tasks. The higher the resistance of the wires and the more current pushed through them, the higher the heat. If bare wire is allowed enough amperes to make it glow red, we can toast bread over it, grill meat, cook soup, etc. If the current is increased a little too much, the wire becomes white hot, it combines with the oxygen in the air, and it simply burns up. This is precisely the action of a fuse in protecting a circuit from an overload of current.

If we want the wire to stay white hot, so that we can illuminate a room with it, we put it in a glass bulb from which the air has been removed, and presto, we have Edison's electric light! Actually, in most lamps larger than 40 watts the air is not only pumped out but is replaced by an inert gas, usually a mixture of nitrogen and argon. This minimizes blackening of the bulb due to bombardment of the internal surface by electrons that boil out of the incandescent filament.

The power formula, *volts x amperes*, applies to heating appliances of various kinds in which only the resistance of the wires is put to work. The wattage rating and the line voltage of most such appliances is marked somewhere on their cases, but the amperage is not always included. It is easy to figure this from the other two values; divide watts by volts and you have amperes. For example, a typical iron marked "1,110 watts, 120 volts" draws a little more than 9 amperes.(The word amperes is frequently shortened to amps.)

There is a common misconception that high voltage means high power. This isn't so; power is any combination of voltage and amperage. A 12-volt automobile lamp that draws 5 amperes is equivalent to a 120-volt house lamp that takes 1/2 ampere; both are 60-watt lamps.

RATINGS OF ELECTRIC MOTORS

As a carryover from the days of horses and steam, electric motors are rated in horsepower rather than wattage. Fortunately, there is a simple relationship; one horsepower is the same as 746 watts. However, you're in for a surprise if you examine the name plate of a typical one-horsepower motor and find that it reads "240 volts AC, 6 amps full load." Multiply 240 by 6 and you get 1,440 watts, no matter how you check your arithmetic. What's wrong?

Nothing. Alternating current behaves differently in motors than it does in toasters and coffee pots. Motors contain large coils of wire

These are some of the transmission lines carrying energy away from the transformers shown on the preceeding page. The lines carry four circuits, each consisting of three wires suspended from insulators.

As the lines fan out from the main circuits, they operate at lower voltages and are smaller than the main lines. The three concrete poles shown carry a single three-phase alternating circuit.

This is a typical pole transformer in a residential area that reduces the overhead line of possibly 2,200 volts to 120-240 volts. This single transformer will usually feed six to ten residences.

that act as electro-magnets and have a property called "inductance" which exists in addition to the inherent resistance of the wire itself. When AC is applied to a machine in which the inductive effect predominates, the current does not flow the instant the voltage comes on, as it does in toasters. Instead, it actually starts a small fraction of a second later; then the two actions are said to be "out of phase." The voltage and the current reach their maximum values at different times in their recurring cycles, so the *average* power of the combination is much lower than when the voltage and current are in phase. To compensate for this lagging action, the current must be increased to bring the effective wattage up to its horsepower equivalent.

LOSSES IN POWER LINES

High resistance is definitely undesirable anywhere in the wiring between the generating station and the furthest outlet in your house. It will make voltage drop off along the way and the heat that builds up in the wire is completely wasted. Compounding this problem is the fact that the lost wattage is equal to the resistance multiplied by the *square* of the current. Thus, for a line resistance of 10 ohms and a current of 5 amps the loss is 10 times 25, or 250 watts. With the same 10 ohms but twice the current, the loss is 10 times 100, or 1,000 watts!

Line losses cannot be eliminated, because all wires have some resistance, but they can be minimized by generating electricity at *high* voltage and low current. A typical power station

might have an output of 10,000 volts. Depending on the distance the juice must travel to its eventual destinations, this might be boosted to 25,000, 50,000 or 100,000 volts. At the water-powered stations, which are usually in remote spots, the line voltage can be as high as 275,000 volts.

THE VERSATILE TRANSFORMER

One of the important features of AC is the ease of transforming it from any voltage to a higher or lower voltage, with great efficiency. The transformers that do this are of simple construction. A basic unit consists of a rectangular framework or core of thin sheets of iron, over which are wound two layers of wire. One winding, called the "primary," connects to the circuit whose voltage is to be changed. From the other, called the "secondary," flows the new voltage; this is in direct proportion to the primary-to-secondary wire winding. It is entirely practical for a single primary to energize several secondaries producing entirely different voltages. For example, a typical radio-TV transformer with a 120-volt primary has three independent secondaries giving 5 volts, 6.3 volts and 1,200 volts.

By the time a power line gets to a residential area it might be running at about 2,000 volts after undergoing several intermediate reductions. The job of the final transformer is to bring this 2,000 volts down to household use. There are often two or three transformers in sight on a single utility pole. These feed different groups of houses, depending on what type and size of electric service is wanted in them. An average pole-mounted transformer is about the size of a 40-gallon garbage can. Larger models are usually installed in underground vaults in the street or on the ground in fenced enclosures.

THE VOLTAGE NUMBERS GAME

Up to about the time of World War II, most small houses were provided with a two-wire, single-phase line from a transformer that delivered 110 volts. Some had a three-wire line that permitted the use of both 110- and 220-volt appliances. During the building boom that followed the war, the public utilities gradually raised the nominal voltage combination of these single-phase circuits to 120/240 volts. Also, to accommodate the big motors of central air-conditioning installations, the utilities brought four-wire, three-phase service into many buildings.

Note carefully that with any three-wire, single-phase service the higher voltage is always exactly double the lower. As shown in an accompanying diagram, 120-volt appliances are connected between the central "ground" wire and either of the outside legs; 240-volt appliances connect only to the two outside legs. The

ground wire really goes to the ground, usually in the form of a buried water pipe.

The three-phase arrangement is quite different. The voltage between the ground and any one of the three "phase legs" is 120 volts but between any pair of phase legs, without the ground, it is 208 volts. Read that again. The voltage combination is 120/208, *not* 120/240.

It is not at all uncommon in housing developments receiving three-phase service to find large homes with the full four-wire deal and smaller ones with a three-wire line. The latter comprises only two of the three phase legs, and while it looks like an ordinary 120/240-volt combination it definitely is not. From ground to either outside wire you have 120 volts, but across the two outside leads it is 208 volts. If you encounter a three-wire service that you can't figure out, for example, in a house that you might want to buy, check with the local public utility and ask questions. You don't want to buy 240-volt appliances and then learn after you install them that you have a 208-volt line!

CONDUCTORS VS. NON-CONDUCTORS

All common metals conduct electricity, some better than others. Silver has the lowest resistance, but because of its cost is used generally only to coat the contact surfaces of switches that carry heavy currents. Copper is very close

Sometimes two or three transformers may be mounted on a single pole to feed several square blocks of houses. And sometimes a single transformer on a pole will only serve a solitary farm.

All the wiring beyond the meter is the responsibility of the home owner. It is sealed by the utility company to discourage tampering and to let you know that there are no fuses inside.

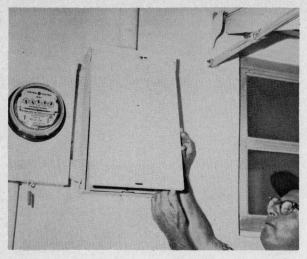

If there is a box next to the meter, you can be pretty sure that it holds either a circuit breaker or a switch. The circuit breaker, or switch, is used to turn off all the current from entire house.

behind, and because it is relatively cheap, highly ductile, and easy to solder, it is used for probably 95 per cent of all electrical wiring. Aluminum is about 50 per cent more resistant than copper, but with its weight advantage—and lower cost—it is useful for many purposes.

Iron has five times the resistance of copper. It is suitable mainly for heating but only at rather low temperatures because it oxidizes rapidly. The wire used almost exclusively for irons, toasters, etc., is Nichrome, an alloy of nickel and chromium.

Metals are generally good conductors because the electrons in them can be set into motion readily by outside influences. The most effective of the latter is ordinary magnetism. A basic alternator consists of hardly more than a round cage of wire in which a magnet rotates. This can be a permanent magnet made of Alnico, a powerful magnetic alloy of aluminum, nickle and cobalt, or it can be an electro-magnet similar to that in a doorbell, energized by a battery or a separate DC generator. The major difference between an alternator at Hoover Dam and the one in your car is size.

Materials having so much resistance that they are absolute non-conductors of electricity are called "insulators" and are used to protect live wires from "short-circuiting" against each other, and also to prevent live people from touching live wires. In this category is a large variety of substances: paper, cotton, wool, glass, ceramics, plastics, silk, nylon and most other man-made fabrics, and air, or no air at all—a vacuum. A highly durable phenolic plastic, Bakelite is a particularly good insulator and has long been a favorite with electrical and radio manufacturers.

A hinged plate covering the box can be swung up revealing a large black handle. Pushing it down, will cut off all the current to the house. Always turn off current before doing any electrical work.

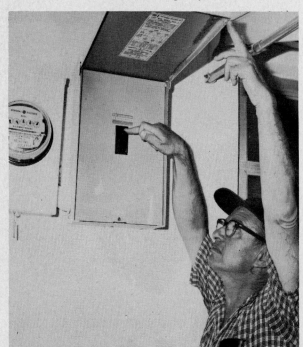

Going a step further, you can pry off the protective cover—after pushing the handle to the Off position—to reveal the heavy cables coming from the meter and leading off to individual branch circuits.

This is what the inside of the switch box looks like after you have removed its cover. The three heavy cables at the left come from the meter, are controlled by the switch, and then lead to the fuse box or circuit breakers.

HOW LONG IS A "SHORT-CIRCUIT?"

At this point you're probably asking, "Just what is a short-circuit?" It's a temporary, accidental and altogether unwelcome connection between exposed wires or other parts of an electrical system. For instance, suppose that the insulation on the line cord of a vacuum cleaner is damaged by careless treatment; the machine is pulled over it, it is stepped on or a dog chews on it. Eventually the bare wires show and are squeezed together the next time the wheels of the cleaner roll over the cord. These touching wires constitute a short-circuit. Because the resistance here is low, the current jumps to high amperage, a lot of heat is generated, and then three events occur at the same time: the joint flares up, the line fuse or circuit breaker kicks open, and the person using the machine gets a bad scare.

A really solid short-circuit like this one is not usually dangerous in the sense that it might start a fire, because the instantaneous current is probably 100 amperes or more, a load that no

fuse or circuit breaker can resist. The sneaky shorts are those whose connections are a bit loose and have enough resistance to heat up appreciably and ignite nearby materials without disengaging the fuse or breaker. Finding and repairing worn wires and similar faults is a vital part of good electrical maintenance and safety in any home.

AC VS. DC

Only scant mention has been made here of direct current because DC house service is a thing of the past. DC is quite different from AC in that it flows steadily in one direction. It is the kind of electricity that comes mainly from batteries. DC is required for many sections of television, radio and related entertainment equipment, and for charging storage batteries in automobiles, photographic flash guns, tape recorders, etc. It is easily obtained in any voltage and amperage from the combination of an AC line transformer and rectifiers connected in the latter's secondary circuit.

How to Read a Meter

The only way to check how much power you are using for any period of time is to read your own meter.

Located outside the home for the convenience of the meter-reader, the size of the conduit leading to the meter often indicates the amperage of the service. This 1-½" pipe means 100 amperes.

Provided by your utility company, this meter is typical of the millions in use that determine what you owe for your electric power. Tamperproof and weathertight, they are rarely replaced.

AT SOME TIME, every home owner has the nagging suspicion that he is paying too much for electricity. His first thought is that the meter is "running fast," but upon honest reflection he will probably realize that the weather has been unusually hot and that his air conditioners have been running almost around the clock.

The easiest way to check on your own power usage is to learn how to read the meter and to keep your own record. You'll still pay according to the monthly record of the power company's "meter maid," but at least you'll become aware of the desirability of conservation habits and you'll teach your family to turn off lights and appliances when they're not really needed.

The most common type of residential meter has a glass cover about six inches in diameter, with four (sometimes five) numbered dials. These look like watch faces, but on closer examination you'll spot two important differences: the numbers go from 0 to 9, not from 1 to 12, and the pointers on adjacent dials turn in opposite directions. The pointers are geared to the drive mechanism (actually, a sort of compound motor that responds to both voltage and current variations) in such a manner that one complete revolution of the right-hand dial moves the pointer of the dial to its immediate

DIGITAL READOUT METER

BETWEEN 8 AND 9 MEANS 8   PAST 2 IS 2   PAST 4 IS 4   NOT YET 2 IS 2 ON LAST DIAL

8242
LAST READING COULD BE—8015
YOU USED IN KILOWATT HRS 227

left one division. Similarly, one complete revolution of the second dial moves the pointer of the third dial one division. The progression continues to the last dial on the left. In other words, the dials are geared in a one-to-ten ratio, corresponding to numbers from 1 to 10 to 100 to 1,000 to 10,000.

READING THE METER

To take a reading, start with the first dial on the left and in each case note the *lower* figure of the two between which the pointer is resting. In the drawing of a four-dial meter, observe that on dial 1 the reading is 8, on dial 2 it is 2, on dial 3 it is 4 and on dial 4 it is 2; this means that a total of 8,242 kilowatt hours of electricity has run through the meter since it was started, assuming that all dials read 0 at that time. If another reading of this meter is made perhaps a week later and the total is 8,674, the consumption for that week was 432 kilowatt hours. Always read a pointer as indicating the figure it passed, not the one to which it is nearer.

If the pointers are too close to the marks on the meter for you to figure them out, wait about half an hour and try again. This problem can't arise with meters of the digital readout type. Just scan the row of numbers and the answer is there! However, not many of these instruments are around—yet.

Typical computer utility bill covering gas and electricity explains all charges to the customer. A indicates the time period and lists actual meter readings from the previous month to the present and B shows the total used for that period. In the case of electric it is in KWH, (which means 1000 watts consumed for one hour). Gas is measured in 100 cubic foot units. With the quantity used recorded, the computer automatically calculates the regular rate (which varies according to the amount and classification) plus a cost-of-fuel adjustment factor as shown in C. Note that D indicates "Est" which means the meter was not actually read by the utility but the use calculated based upon previous usage. Some utilities offer a budget plan which means adveraging the estimated yearly total and dividing by 12. In this way a 20-dollar heating bill of June is balanced by a 80-dollar December bill. The computer keeps track of all charges, as shown in E, and at the end of the year an adjustment is made. Ask your utility to explain all charges, rates, classifications, adjustments etc. so you know what you are paying for and how much electric or gas used.

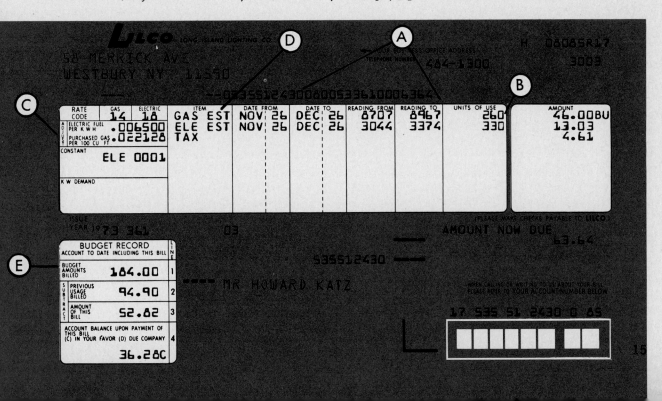

In a small house or apartment, the fuse box is generally installed in the wall of a hallway or even in a closet. In large private homes, it will be found in the garage, a stair well, or in basement.

In an all-electric house you will find circuit breakers instead of fuses, mounted inside of a steel box as shown. It is a good idea to identify each circuit according to the room or area it serves.

Fuses vs. Circuit Breakers

Both protect you from line overloads that could result in fire and burned out motors. But the circuit breaker makes life much easier.

"WHICH ARE BETTER—fuses or circuit breakers? This question is asked repeatedly by prospective buyers of new houses as well as owners of old houses.

The answer depends on circumstances. If a real short-circuit develops in a defective appliance, the line fuse will blow out or the breaker will trip open with the same speed, thus protecting the line against potential fire danger. You unplug the appliance and go to the branch panel to restore the line. If the panel contains fuse sockets, you must, obviously, have a replacement for the dead fuse. But do you? When did you last check your supply, and do you remember where you put it? The answers to these questions can sometimes be downright embarrassing. However, if the branch panel contains circuit breakers you can approach it with a smile on your face, because breakers look exactly like ordinary switches and you can reset the tripped unit merely by pushing its little handle to the "on" position. So chalk up "convenience" as an advantage for the circuit breaker.

TYPES OF FUSES

There are two different kinds of screw-in fuses of identical appearance. The first, marked "slow-blow," gets its name from its ability to remain intact on a *momentary* over-load in excess of its rated capacity. It was designed specifically for machines such as clothes washers, air conditioners and stationary power tools, whose motors take a heavy current for perhaps a second after they are started and then drop quickly to their normal running current. If a

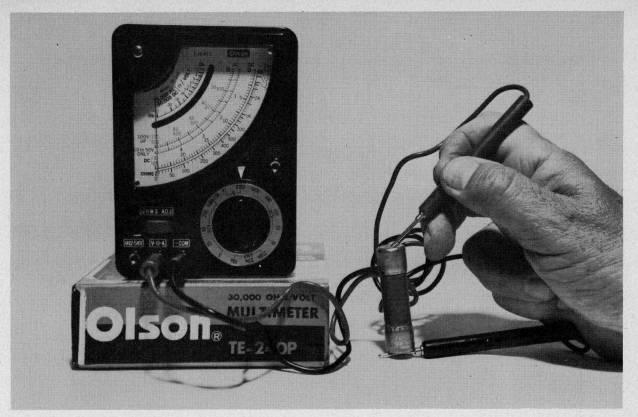

The only way to determine the condition of a suspected cartridge-type fuse is to run a continuity check with a multimeter. There is no visible evidence of failure or "good" with fuses of this kind.

The pencil points to the contact spring in the bottom of the circuit breaker that connects to the "hot" side of the current-feeding plate in the breaker box. Breakers for 240 volts have two contacts.

A typical twin circuit breaker for two 120-volt circuits. The finger points to the trip handles. The "hot" black wires connect to screw terminals at the bottom of the insulated circuit breaker case.

Non-Tamp fuses in standard amperage ratings, have varying base diameters, are not interchangeable, and screw into individual adapters that screw in turn into the regular fuse sockets in the fuse box.

machine is overloaded and the motor cannot achieve its rated speed, the continuing heavy current will blow the fuse as a warning to the owner.

An ordinary fuse, (not a slow-blow) is suitable for other household appliances such as lights, dishwashers, disposals, fans, sewing machines, radio/hi-fi/TV equipment, etc., but it is not practical for the heavier machines because it blows almost the instant the switch is turned on. Of course, slow-blows can be used for all purposes, and for this reason many electrical supply catalogs don't even list the ordinary kind. All standard circuit breakers have the delayed-trip feature built in, another point in their favor.

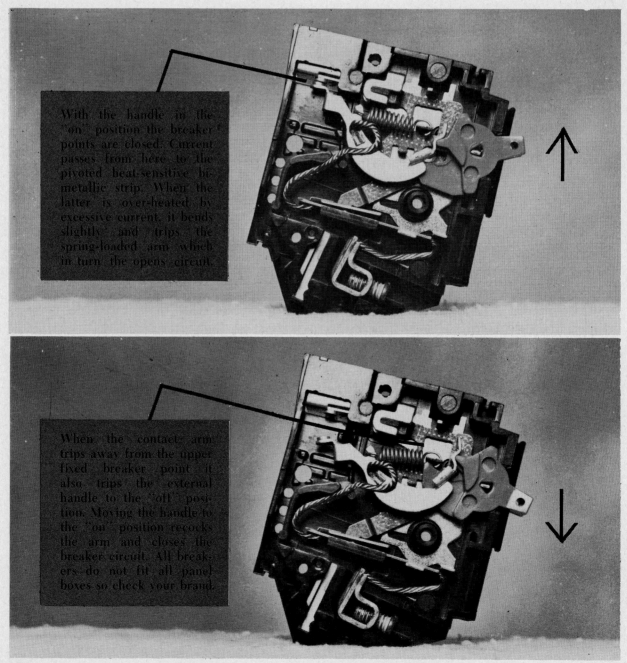

With the handle in the "on" position the breaker points are closed. Current passes from here to the pivoted heat-sensitive bi-metallic strip. When the latter is over-heated by excessive current, it bends slightly and trips the spring-loaded arm which in turn the opens circuit.

When the contact arm trips away from the upper fixed breaker point it also trips the external handle to the "off" position. Moving the handle to the "on" position recocks the arm and closes the breaker circuit. All breakers do not fit all panel boxes so check your brand.

The inside of a breaker box for an all-electric house is a maze of heavy wires for 15 separate circuits. Five for 240 volts and ten for 120 volts. Finger points to a common buss to which all the white wires (the grounds) are connected. Caution: keep fingers away far from all exposed terminals holding heavy cables from meter and main.

DISADVANTAGE OF FUSES

From the protective standpoint, a weakness of the fuse system is the ease with which it can be manipulated dangerously by an unthinking home owner. In older houses the capacity of most branch circuits is 15 amperes, whereas in newer models it is likely to be 20. If a 15-ampere fuse blows now and then with too many appliances on the line, some people don't hesitate to screw in a 20-amp plug instead. And if this pops out, they'll even try a 25-amp fuse. It doesn't seem to occur to them that they are putting a slow match to their own property.

If you know anyone so foolish, try to sell him on the idea of using Non-Tamp fuses. These resemble regular fuses, but have slightly smaller bodies whose diameters depend on the current rating. They are sold with reducing adapters that go into the fuse sockets, and once in they cannot be unscrewed without virtually breaking the fuse socket. A 15-amp adapter accommodates only a 15-amp Non-Tamp, a 20-amp size only a 20-amp Non-Tamp, etc., and no nonsense about it! These fuses also have the desirable slow-blow action.

CIRCUIT BREAKERS

Breakers for 120-volt circuits are made either as singles or as pairs in one case, with sepa-

rate on-off handles. For 240-volt lines they are always paired, with a joined handle. Thus, regardless of which half tends to open first on an overload, because of slight differences in manufacturing tolerances, the two sections flip open together and the defective appliance is completely disconnected from the line. With fuses, there is always the possibility that one of the pair required for 240-volt applications will remain intact after the other blows. This means that one side of the 240-volt appliance is still "hot" with 120 volts.

The internal arrangement of a breaker box is fairly easy to understand. With a standard three-wire, 120/240-volt service, the two "hot" cables (one red and one black or both black) terminate under two heavy clamps at the top center of the enclosure. The mounting plates under the clamps are stagger-cut and well insulated from each other, and have short ears to engage the contacts of the individual breakers. The spacing of the ears is such that only 240-volt breakers fit across the two hot sides of the circuit, and only 120-volt breakers connect between the hot side and the common ground. There is no way of making errors here, as the breakers simply cannot be made to fit where they do not belong. The white or bare ground cable of the incoming service and all of the white wires of the branch circuits are connected to a common "buss" on the inner wall of the box.

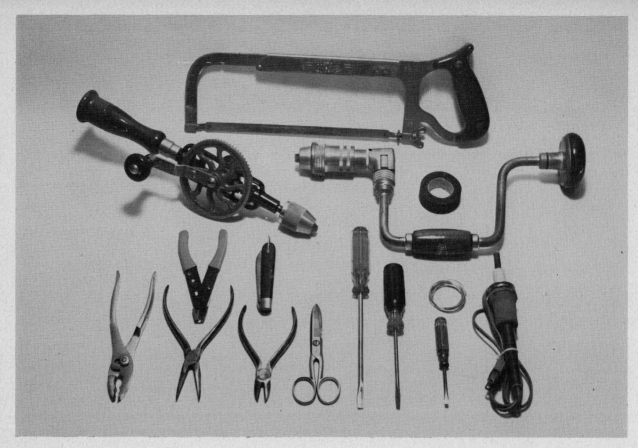

The common hand tools shown above should enable you to take care of most of the small electrical repair jobs around the house. When you buy any of these tools, buy best for a lifetime investment.

Tools and Testing

Making electrical repairs requires far fewer tools than carpentry, plumbing or masonry. But the right tools will make the job easier.

PRACTICALLY all the small jobs of maintenance and repair of household electrical appliances, installation of new fixtures, and wiring new outlets can be done with the hand tools and supplies that normally accumulate in the basement or garage.

Check the contents of your tool box and see how many of the items shown in the photographs you already have.

Slip-joint pliers. Also known as gas pliers. For twisting heavy wires, holding parts to be soldered, undoing or tightening nuts, bending sheet metal, etc. The inner surfaces of the jaws are ribbed and slightly concave; they can grip rods and pipes up to about 5/8th inch in diameter.

Long-nose pliers. For twisting wires under the heads of terminal screws on plugs, outlets, soc-

kets, and for holding small parts. The tips must close tightly so they can pick up and maintain their grip on thin wires, soldering lugs, washers, etc. An urgent caution about this tool: use it only for light work, never for tightening nuts. Some long-nose pliers have wire-cutting jaws near the joint.

Side-cutters. For the sole purpose of snipping wire. The angled cutting lips come to a fine point, so they can cut very close. If you use side-cutters only on copper or aluminum wire, they will last a lifetime. If you tighten nuts with them, they'll quickly lose their cutting edges and their alignment. It's almost impossible to repair a damaged tool of this type. Buy a new one and treat it properly this time.

Wire-stripper. Replaces the common knife as a means of removing insulation from wires without nicking them. Resembles side-cutters, but can be adjusted quickly to bite only through the insulation and to stop at the wire. A great time saver.

Pocket knife. For scraping wires clean and shiny. Use the *back* edge of the blade, not the sharp side. If you're in the market for a new knife, look in surplus stores for the Army's TL-29. This is a sturdy tool with one regular blade and one combination scraper-screwdriver blade. The latter locks in its open position.

Short, stout scissors. For cutting tape, trimming insulation, forming thin washers, etc.

Screwdrivers. Three are shown here, but you'll need probably three or four more of the Phillips cross-head type. You can touch up the tips of flat screwdrivers with a few strokes of a file, but there's almost nothing you can do with the Phillips type once their points have been mangled.

In the absence of a Phillips of the correct size, you can often get by if you have a small grinder and can shape the end of a common screwdriver to fit across and into one slot of the recessed head of a particular Phillips screw. The fit should be snug; if it isn't, the blade will chew away the corners of the slot.

Soldering iron. You have a wide choice. For most electrical connections, the pencil type with screw-in tips is inexpensive and adequate. Incidentally, the word "iron" means tool. The working end of a soldering iron is always made of copper. Irons of the "gun" type are popular

This wire stripper takes the pain out of the job of removing insulation without cutting the wire. Here the jaws are being adjusted to match diameter of the wire to be stripped for connection.

The wire is placed between the jaws, the handles are squeezed and then pulled toward the end of the wire—and off comes the insulation. Too narrow an opening will cut or nick the wire.

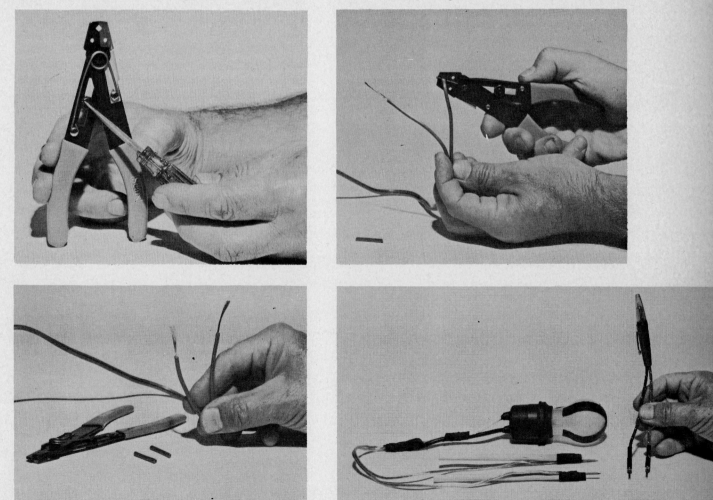

In less time than it takes you to read this caption, you will have two neatly stripped wires. Avoid excessive handling of the stripped wires if you are planning to make a soldered connection.

Two simple "hot-line" checkers. At left is a home-made model consisting of 10-watt lamp in a socket with nails connected to dowels for prods. Right, commercial neon lamp with short test prods.

because they heat to operating temperature in only about three seconds. However, they tend to be heavy.

Solder. For electrical work use only rosin-core solder. This produces clean joints with no corrosive after-effect. Under no circumstances use acid-core solder because its flux residue quickly attacks the wire.

Brace. With an assortment of bits, essential for boring holes in floors, ceilings and walls for wires.

Tape. For covering splices in wires and reinforcing insulation on flexible cords of appliances. The usual kind is black and is called friction tape, but plastic tape, which costs a little more, holds tighter. Ordinary adhesive tape made for medical purposes is also very good as are clear, colored or *Scotch* tape.

Hand drill. Or a small electric drill. For general hole-making.

Hack saw. For cutting flexible armored cable and similar jobs.

Not shown in the illustration are such basic tools as a hammer, saw, ladder and wrenches, which are familiar to homeowners who do their own maintenance chores.

MAKE A TESTER

You can tell if a plug fuse (the screw-in type) is intact or blown by just looking at it, but something more than observation is needed to check a cartridge fuse. You can't tell by just looking at an appliance cord whether the wires inside are short-circuited or broken. You can't tell from looking whether a bare, exposed wire is "hot" or not, although you can tell very definitely if you are foolish enough to touch it. For serious trouble-shooting you need an electrical tool called simply a "tester".

If you have a lamp socket and a piece of lamp cord 10 or 12 inches long you can make a perfectly good "hot-line" tester in about 15 minutes. Connect one end of the cord to the socket. Solder the wires at the other end to two common nails about 1½ inches long with their heads cut off. Cut two ½-inch dowels or similar round sticks, and tape the soldered nails to their ends, leaving about a half-inch sticking out. These insulated handles are called "probes."

Take a small 15-watt bulb and screw it into the socket. To minimize shattering if it strikes something hard, put a couple of strips of tape across the glass. To check if this tester is ready for testing, push the probes into the slots of a live outlet, and note if the bulb lights. It would be helpful to have the socket switch "on". Hold

the sticks at their free ends, and you can now poke around live 120-volts circuits safely.

BUY A TESTER

For less than a dollar you can buy a tester that looks like a fountain pen with a couple of short wires coming out of one end. Inside is a small neon lamp that glows bright red when the bare tips on the wire are touched to any live house circuit. A handy gadget.

A hot-line tester can tell you positively if the circuit to an outlet is properly grounded. Examine the parallel slots in the outlet closely and you will note that one is wider than the other. This wide one is—or should be—connected to the white, current-carrying grounded wire inside the box. Poke one probe into this slot and touch the other to the cover plate or the center mounting screw. If these are painted over, the contact may not be good, so remove the screw, pry off the plate, and repeat the test with the second probe touching the steel box from which the screw was removed. The lamp should *not* light because the box is also grounded and there can be no complete circuit in what is, in effect, one wire.

TESTING FOR GROUND

Now shift the first probe to the narrower slot and again put the second probe on the box; the test light should come on immediately. But suppose it doesn't? This is a sure sign that the grounding wire is not continuous between the box and the actual ground connection near the meter and the entrance switch. This connection is usually made to the water pipe entering the house near the electric service line.

Interruption of the grounding of armored cable or conduit is almost impossible because the path is continuous as the various sections are clamped to boxes for switches, outlets and lights.

The hot-line tester is also useful for a quick check on the circuits from the fuse or circuit breaker box. It sometimes reveals pretty silly cases of "trouble". To get at the actual live terminals in the box, you will have to remove a punched plate that covers the fuses or breakers and leaves only their tops or handles in sight. Usually this means only loosening a couple of screws.

Look before you touch. Whether you have two- or three-wire service, note that all the white wires are connected to a common ground strip, and that the fuses or breakers are inserted only in the black or red lines.

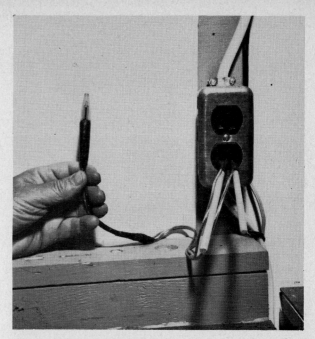

If the wires of the neon tester shown on the preceeding page are lengthened and fitted with probes as above, the device is easier and safer to use on live circuits. Handle it only by the dowel ends.

The neon tester will light up on any voltage between 60 and 500 volts. When the probes are pushed into the slots of 120-volt outlet, neon bulb will glow bright red, showing circuit is live.

TESTING CIRCUITS

To acquaint yourself with the circuits, start with the heavy wires that come from the meter or the main switch. The white one will join the other whites. With two-wire service there is one heavy black lead; with three-wire, two heavy black leads (or one black and one red). If you have the home-made test lamp, touch one probe to the ground strip and the other to the single black or to the two blacks individually. There are 120 volts between any of these points and ground, so the lamp will light to show that the service is normal. If you touch the probes of the test lamp to the two black points of a three-wire service it will probably burn out in a second or two, because the voltage here is 208 volts or more likely 240. With the neon tester, however, this test can be performed without damage to the bulb.

If the loose probe is touched to both sides of a fuse or breaker in turn, with the first probe still grounded, the tester will light up each time. If the fuse is blown (a condition you can simulate by merely removing it) it will light on one side but not on the other. It often happens that a fuse appears to be okay with the internal element clean and shiny, yet the tester does not light up when it should. Perhaps you will unscrew the fuse, note that it still looks good, put it back, make another check, and then discover to your surprise that the tester now does light

up! How come? The only possible explanation is that the fuse was a trifle loose in its socket. This might have been caused by the vibration of a nearby washing machine, furnace blower, air conditioner, etc.

CIRCUIT BREAKERS

Circuit breakers are much less susceptible to trouble than fuses, but even they must be regarded with a little suspicion. In a new house fitted with an elaborate breaker box, I once spent a frantic and frustrating half-hour trying to figure out why an inoffensive-looking outlet in the nearby garage refused to show any sign of life. I was about to disconnect the whole line and pull it through its conduit when I stopped to catch my breath. In desperation and pique, I started to flip the breakers back and forth a couple of times, and when I hit the last one in the first row I couldn't believe my eyes when I saw my test light in the outlet flash on. The fault was that the breaker needed just an extra little nudge to snap the inside contacts closed! As in all trouble-shooting work, the moral is: think of the simple, obvious things first. If I'd checked the outlet side of the breaker's black wire I'd have saved time and temper.

CONTINUITY TESTING

There is another type of tester called the "continuity checker". This too looks like a fountain pen, but it contains one or two small flashlight cells in addition to a small lamp connected to a pair of test leads like those on the neon light. It is intended primarily to distinguish between a short-circuit and an open circuit; for example, to tell if a fuse is intact or open, or if the contacts of a switch have welded together or broken off, or if wires enclosed in a common sheath of insulation have shorted together or broken. The lamp merely lights when the circuit is closed or, doesn't light when it is open.

CAUTION: never use a continuity checker of any kind on a live circuit, or anything connected to one. With appliances or machines having flexible line cords, *always* pull the plug first and then think about a test procedure. If a suspected component is soldered or otherwise connected, undo the connections to isolate it from other parts that might give misleading indications on the tester.

The basic continuity checker is of limited or no value with appliances or devices that normally have some appreciable resistance. When this resistance is interposed between the battery and the lamp, the maximum current that can flow isn't enough, in many cases, to light the lamp. Whether the appliance is okay or defective, the lamp stays out. For example, a fan having the relatively low resistance of 50 ohms would just about make the lamp glow if the batteries were fresh, but a clock with a resistance of 800 ohms would positively prevent it from lighting.

THE MULTIMETER

For really informative continuity checking, the kind that might save you or members of your family from nasty shocks—or worse—you should invest about $15 in a modest "multimeter." This does more than just light up; it actually measures the resistance of the wires in an appliance or of the accidental bridging of "hot" wires to its metal frame, a near-grounding con-

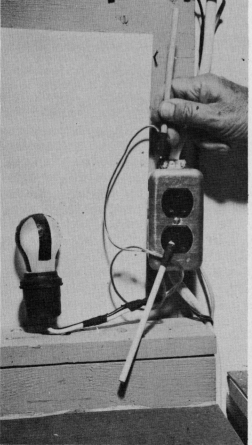

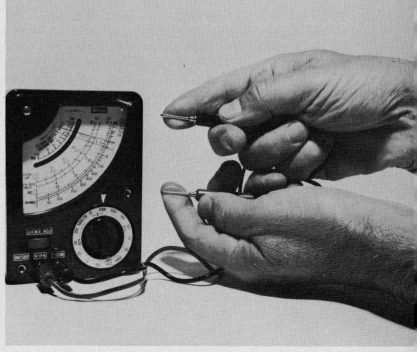

Is this outlet properly ground? Is it live? Checking it with either style tester will quickly tell you the answer. Note how probe is handled by the insulated end.

The versatile multimeter is invaluable for checking continuity of circuits, parts, resistance, and general trouble-shooting. The one shown above costs about $18.

dition that is really dangerous.

The instrument is called a multimeter because in one small package it combines the functions of an ohmmeter, a voltmeter and an ammeter (that is, ampere-meter). The meter shown in the accompanying illustrations is representative of the large assortment on the market, at prices ranging from about $8 to $100. It measures resistance all the way to 6,000,000 ohms, AC voltage to 1,000 volts, DC voltage to 2,500 volts, and small direct current to ¼ ampere. It is extremely versatile as it can be used to shoot trouble in almost any device that runs on electricity: appliances, radios, televisions, hi-fi systems, recorder equipment, automobile ignition systems, electric trains, flash guns, etc. It more than pays for itself the first time it enables you to detect a potentially dangerous situation.

A case very much in point concerns an electric hot-pot used by one of my neighbors for preparing quick soup lunches. Entering my garage shop with the utensil in her hands, she said "The last time I used this thing I got a strong tingling sensation when I touched it. My husband told me to throw it out right away, but I thought you might look at it first."

Tingling sensation indeed! Quite clearly there was internal electrical leakage between the aluminum case and either the heating element or the connections to it. I connected one probe of the multimeter to the case and the other to one of the prongs of the line plug, and noted that the needle immediately started to waver around the 13,000 ohm mark on the scale. If there has been no leakage, the needle would have remained absolutely still, indicating *no* internal connection. I disconnected the probes and picked up the pot and then I *heard* the cause of the trouble—it was the sound of liquid rolling around inside. As I unscrewed the bottom section of the pot, several ounces of water poured out. Reassembled, the pot now showed the right resistance reading on the meter, so it could now be used safely.

The ability of a multimeter to reveal dangerous leakage is what makes the instrument such a valuable tool. *Any* measurable resistance between the metal case of an appliance and the line cord is bad and becomes worse as the resistance decreases to zero—a dead short-circuit.

Sensitivity of the multimeter is put to good use in determining why this electric pot produced a shock. The answer: An internal connection between the shell and the wiring. What caused leakage? Bottom of can was full of water!

Successful Soldering

**A well-soldered splice is the best guarantee
of a foolproof electrical connection.**

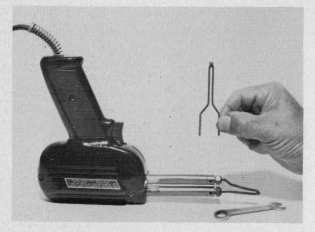

It is easy to see why this is called a gun-type soldering iron—it has a trigger, like a gun, to turn on the heat. The copper wire tips can be removed by loosening the two nuts at each end.

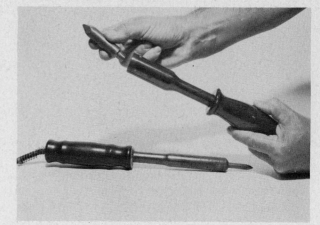

Two regular irons for general work. The smaller one, rated at 85 watts, has a plain shank, copper tip held in place with a setscrew. Larger iron, 150 watts, has a tip that is screwed into the body.

SOLDERING is a highly useful operation that you can master with five minutes of practice if you observe a very simple precaution: *Cleanliness.* Your fingers should be clean and dry, so that you don't transfer skin oil to the work being soldered; the metal surfaces that are to be joined must be clean, clear and bright, with no trace of insulation or other previous covering; and the tip of the soldering tool (the iron) must have a shiny coat of simmering solder.

"Solder" is a soft alloy, generally of 60 per cent lead and 40 per cent tin. The type universally used for electrical purposes is in the form of hollow wire, filled with rosin. The latter is called "flux" and its job is to absorb oxidation products of the metal being soldered as it gets hot enough to melt the solder. Without flux of some kind the molten solder will not adhere to the joint, but merely forms globules that roll away like so many drops of water on a waxed surface.

Both copper and brass (an alloy of copper and zinc) are very receptive to soldering with rosin flux.

Soldering tools are usually called "irons,"

although the term is a misnomer as the heated tip that does the actual work is a piece of copper. The heat is provided by a coil of resistance within the body of the tool. Depending on size, a straight iron takes from about three to five minutes to reach operating temperature.

Irons are rated by their power consumption in watts. The light-weight, pencil-type iron consumes about 50 watts and uses a variety of screw-in tips with bases like those on Christmas tree bulbs. It is inexpensive, and is entirely satisfactory for 95 per cent of household electrical repair work. Larger models run to 85 and 150 watts.

Soldering tools that look like pistols are called "soldering guns" are popular with many men (and women!) because they heat up in a matter of seconds instead of minutes. They are in effect small transformers, with a primary winding of many turns of fine wire connected to the AC power line through a trigger switch on the handle. The secondary winding consists of one or two turns of very heavy wire or tubing. The ends of the secondary are joined by a U-shaped loop of copper wire about 1/8-inch square. The step-down action of the transform-

 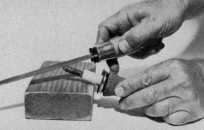 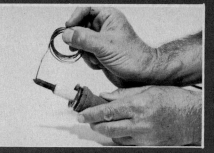

1. Strip away the insulation from ends of the wire, an inch or so is fine. Use steel wool to brighten the wire ends.

2. Clean the iron by rubbing it with steel wool or a fine file. Make sure that all surfaces have been thoroughly cleaned.

3. Tin the iron by applying some solder to the hot iron. It should flow freely over the entire surface of cleaned, hot iron.

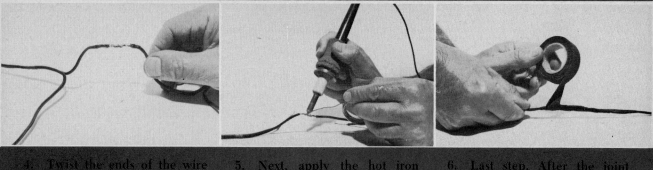

4. Twist the ends of the wire together as shown. A little flux applied to your fingers will keep the wires extra clean.

5. Next, apply the hot iron and some solder, to the joint. The solder should flow readily around the twisted wire joint.

6. Last step. After the joint has cooled, apply insulating tape. Apply tape equal to the thickness of original insulation.

er produces a low secondary voltage but the current in amperes is high enough to heat the loop quickly to soldering temperature. Tips eventually burn up, and are easily replaceable. A typical gun is rated at 100 watts.

Each time a soldering iron is to be used, it must be "tinned." First clean the tip by rubbing it on emery cloth or with a fine file. Plug it into an outlet, and while it is warming up hold the solder against the point. Some of the flux will run down, followed by molten solder. Let it cook for a few seconds until the flux smoke disappears. Wipe the tip with a clean rag and you are ready to work.

The accompanying pictures show what is probably the commonest electrical soldering job —splicing two pieces of lamp cord. It should take you less time to do this than to read the instructions.

Here are some useful do's and don'ts:

● After allowing several drops to melt onto a joint, remove the solder but keep the iron in position for a few seconds, to cook out excess rosin. Remove the iron, but don't disturb the joint for another few seconds. This gives the solder a chance to set thoroughly. If you jiggle the wire too soon, the joint will become undone. Start again, please.

● Always position the joint so that the molten solder runs into or along it, not away from it. Hot solder flows as readily as water.

● Keep your fingers away from the joint; it gets *very* hot, and a solder burn can be nasty. If you must hold the two parts of a joint to keep them from separating, use a pair of pliers (locking type pliers are good) or a spring-type wooden clothespin.

● Don't try to solder aluminum or stainless steel with the same solder and flux used for copper and brass. These metals require special solders and fluxes, and the results are not always fully satisfactory. Iron is a little less troublesome, but it needs an acid-base flux that tends to be very corrosive. And never use an acid-base flux for electrical work.

● The insulation on some wires is a flexible plastic that loosens or burns in the presence of a hot soldering iron. Don't let this bother you. After the joint cools, you'll have to tape it anyway.

Electrical Supplies and Replacement Parts

The electrical section of your local hardware store, home center or department store has a wide variety of parts for every job. And if you can't find what you need, here are some ideas.

THE ELECTRICAL PARTS that need normal replacement are readily available. Light bulbs, fluorescent starters, fuses, cords and plugs, switches, outlets, etc., can be found not only in electrical supply and hardware stores but also in supermarkets, department stores, drug stores, and discount houses. In many classified telephone directories there are listings for firms that cater to home owners. A typical one reads, "Appliance Parts Center—Do-It-Yourself —Complete stock of parts for all makes and models of major appliances." It's worth visiting such a store just to see what's there that you might need sometime.

SPECIAL PARTS

A problem might develop if a particular part of a machine breaks or wears away and a replacement is not obtainable locally. What to do? Examine the machine carefully for the name and address of the manufacturer, a model number and possibly a serial number; play it safe and record *all* the numbers you can find. Write to the factory, marking the letter: Atten-tion—Service Manager. Describe the needed part as well as you can, and if possible include a sketch of it. Also give the approximate date of your purchase and the name and address of the dealer. This information might be helpful, as different production runs of machines are often shipped to different parts of the country. Some manufacturers do not like to deal directly with owners of their products, and may refer you to a distributor in your area. If the item you need is small, some manufacturers might send you a free replacement. They figure that the resulting good will is worth more than the bookkeeping involved in a sales transaction.

THE STORE OF LAST RESORT

As a last resort, try visiting local junk shops and look for discarded machines that you might be able to cannibalize. These places are sometimes real treasure lodes. Take along a few wrenches, pliers and screwdrivers, as you may have to dig out the part yourself. However, before you start, settle the price with the yard owner, to avoid arguments later.

Basic electrical supplies show above are: 1—Twin light socket. 2—Flat triple connector. 3—Three-outlet rubber cube tap. 4—Three-light lamp modernizer. 5—Standard appliance connector. 6—Six-ft. replacement cord. 7—Bar-type bell push button. 8—Round bell push button. 9—Bottom turn-knob socket. 10—Lighted doorbell button. 11—Doorbell buzzer. 12— Chime transformer, 16 volt. 13—Friction tape. 14—Wire connector. 15—Cord clip. 16—Lamp harp. 17—Two-in. switch box. 18—Two-and-one-quarter-inch switch box. 19—Two-and-one-half-inch switch box. 20- Switch box with bracket. 21—Four-inch octagon box. 22–Utility box. 23—Utility cover. 24—Round box cover. 25—Cable connector. 26—Armored cable straps. 27- Non-tamp fuse plug. 28— Fustat plug. 29—Fustat adapter. 30—Glass fuse plug. 31—One-time cartridge fuse. 32— Weatherproof floodlight holder. 33—Disneyland night lights. 34—Pigtail lamp holder. 35—Double safety receptacle. 36—Grounding receptacle on a four-inch cover. 37—Double-grounding receptacle. 38—Single-grounding receptacle. 39—Round grip plug. 40— Porcelain pony cleat lampholder. 41—Pull-chain coiling lampholder side outlet. 42— Combination switch & outlet plate.

What You Should Know About Incandescent Bulbs

The ordinary light bulb is really not ordinary. It is a brilliantly engineered "appliance" that is being constantly improved.

THE COMMON INCANDESCENT lamp is the simplest and most widely used of all electrical "appliances," so you should know a little about its construction.

Let's start with the filament, as shown in the accompanying illustration. This is a length or coil of tungsten wire, heated to incandescence (whiteness) by electric current flowing through it. Coiling the filament increases its light-producing efficiency; forming a coiled-coil raises it further.

Filling Gas. Usually a mixture of nitrogen and argon, which is inert. This reduces evaporation of the tungsten filament and allows higher temperature operation, thus improving the brilliance of the light. Used in most lamps of 40-

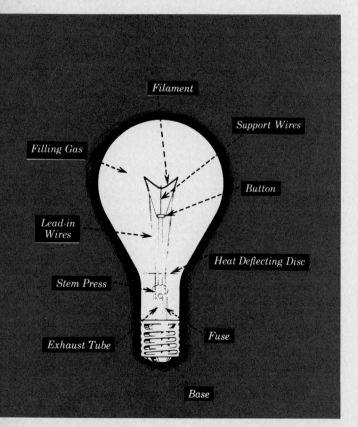

New lamps are being constantly developed not only for longer life, but to produce the same brightness with reduced wattage. This is one great area of research to conserve electricity.

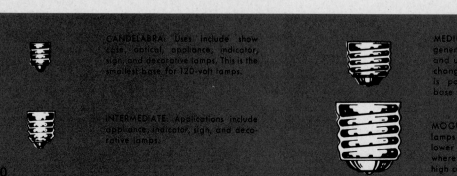

CANDELABRA: Uses include show case, optical, appliance, indicator, sign, and decorative lamps. This is the smallest base for 120-volt lamps.

MEDIUM: This base is standard on general service lamps of 300 watts and under. A high degree of interchangeability in lamp applications is possible because the medium base is so widely used.

INTERMEDIATE: Applications include appliance, indicator, sign, and decorative lamps.

MOGUL: Normally used on 300-watt lamps and up. Also applied on special lower wattage lamps, particularly where low voltage design means a high current.

watt rating and higher.

Lead-In Wires. Electrically connect the filament to the lamp base. From the latter to the stem press they are made of copper; from the stem press to the filament, of nickel.

Stem Press. Supports the filament assembly. Glass and lead-in wires are sealed airtight here.

Exhaust Tube. During manufacture this projects beyond the bulb. Through it, the air in the bulb is pumped out and replaced by filling gas. The tube is then sealed off short enough for the base to fit over it.

Support Wires. These hold the filament in place and protect it during shipment and handling, they are made of molybdenum. A minimum number are used, because they drain off some of the heat of the filament and reduce lamp efficiency.

Button. Holds the filament support wires.

Heat Deflecting Disc. Reduces the flow of hot gases from near the filament into the neck of the bulb. Thus, it protects the stem press, stem and socket from excessive temperatures. Used in higher-wattage general-service lamps.

Fuse. Quickly removes voltage from the filament if the latter arcs over. This reduces metal sputtering and prevents the bulb from cracking.

Base. Screw type. Connects the lamp to the electric circuit and permits easy lamp replacement. Made of either brass or aluminum.

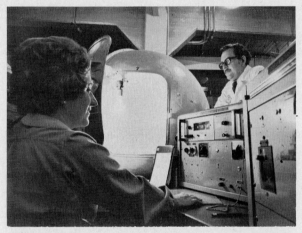

This Westinghouse engineer is about to measure the lumen count—or brightness—of their 3000 hour bulb. The increased life is due to use of krypton gas rather than nitrogen and argon.

CURRENT RATINGS OF HOUSEHOLD BULBS			
6 watts ... .050 amp.		75 watts .... .63 amp.	
10 " .... .083 "		100 " ... .83 "	
25 " .... .21 "		150 " ... 1.25 "	
40 " .... .34 "		200 " ... 1.67 "	
60 " .... .50 "		300 " ... 2.50 "	

SKIRTED: Used on lamps where the neck is too large to fit into the desired size base, or where additional space between the filament and lamp terminals is desired.

BAYONET: Applied on specialty lamps, such as, for vacuum cleaners, sewing machines, etc. Also used on low-voltage lamps.

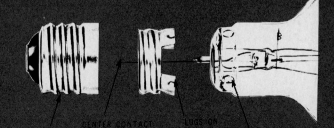

BRASS SCREW BASE

CENTER CONTACT LEAD-IN WIRE

LUGS ON INNER SHELL

MATCH RECESSES IN GLASS BULB

NO CEMENT IS USED

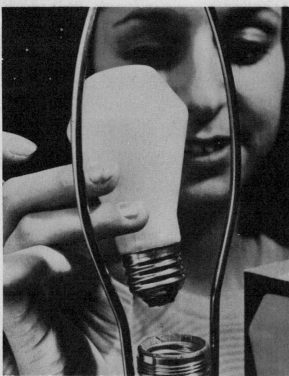

This new Westinghouse bulb, available in 60, 75 and 100-watt sizes, uses   krypton and is reputed to have an average life of 3000 hours. Normal bulbs have a life of approximately 1000 hours.

This Westinghouse testing facility is researching a new line of bulbs called Econ-O-Watt. Designed to consume approximately 25 percent less power than conventional lamps, they cost more.

General Electric alone makes more than 70 types of glass bulb shapes and sizes. They are designated by two-part abbreviations. The first, a letter, indicates the shape. For instance, A stands for the familiar teardrop shape used in most household lamps. Various other standard shapes are also shown.

The second part of the designation expresses the maximum diameter of the bulb in eighths of an inch. Thus, the R-40, a popular style for photographic and general lighting, is a reflector bulb with a diameter of about five inches (40 eighths).

While people generally think of incandescents in terms of white light, there are many decorative applications using colored lamps. Consider the possibilities of G E *Coloramics* in such hues as sun gold, dawn pink, spring green and sky blue! These are available in four wattages: 75, 100, 150 and 50/100/150, the last for "three-way" fixtures.

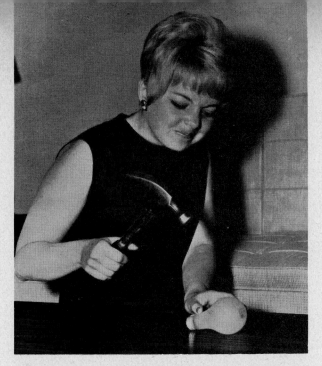 

This bulb will not break if dropped or hit by a hammer because it has a tough silicone rubber coating. It is four times as tough as an ordinary bulb and has a special rough-service filament.

These new mercury vapor bulbs provide a simple means for industrial and commercial users to save electricity and increase illumination. They pioneered the smaller household mercury lamps.

 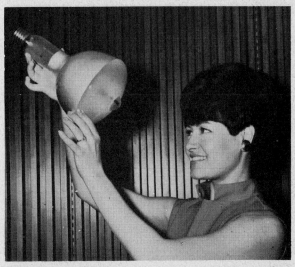

Infrared heat bulbs are popular in the bathroom, but heretofor were very large. This new Westinghouse bulb is only 3¾" in diameter but delivers the same amount of heat as larger units.

You now can use the same fixtures and enjoy the longer life and added light benefits of mercury vapor lamps with this new 750-watt bulb by Westinghouse because it has a built-in ballast.

Below: This small (5" long) mercury vapor bulb designed for household use has 12 times the life and produces twice the light of ordinary bulbs. Compare it with the large industrial bulb.

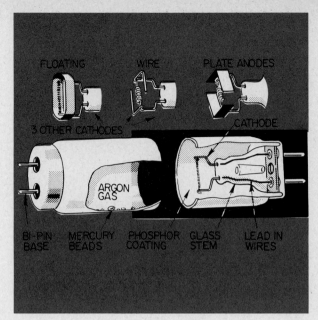

Left: In addition to a recessed light over the counter, this kitchen has a completely fluorescent ceiling. Strips of 40-watt fixtures are attached to ceiling new gridwork is dropped 8".

Fluorescents-the Modern Light Source

Fluorescent fixtures cost more than comparable incandescent but produce the same light at 1/3 the cost. Bulbs last 8-12 times longer.

INCANDESCENT LAMPS consist of a wire filament inside a glass bulb. Fluorescents are entirely different in construction, operation and appearance. The first illustration shows their basic internal arrangement, common to all types. The components are as follows:

1. A glass tube, or bulb, internally coated with fluorescent material called phosphors. 2. Electrodes called "cathodes," supported by a glass mount structure, and sealed at the ends of the tube. 3. A filling gas to aid starting and operation—usually argon, or argon with neon. 4. A small amount of mercury which vaporizes during lamp operation. 5. A base cemented on each end of the tube to connect the lamp to the lighting circuit.

Tube. Acts as an airtight enclosure for the mercury, the filling gas, the cathodes, and the phosphor coating. Glass must be free of structural defects and cleaned before lamp assembly.

Bases. Connect the lamp to the electric circuit, and support the lamp. Lamps for preheat and rapid start circuits use two contacts on each end of the lamp. The bipin base is used on all preheat and many rapid start lamps. Some rapid start type lamps, such as high output and *Power Groove* lamps, use recessed double contact bases because of the higher ballast voltage required with lamps longer than 4 feet. Instant start lamps require only one electrical contact on each end of the lamp; thus the single-pin base is most commonly used. Some instant start lamps use bipin bases with the two contacts connected together inside the lamps.

Mount Structures. Close off ends of the tube and support each cathode. Wires leading from base are sealed off here. These wires are made of special metal, called Dumet wire, which has virtually the same coefficient of expansion as glass. The mount structure also includes a long glass exhaust tube; during manufacture, air is pumped out of the bulb, and the filling gas and mercury are inserted. The exhaust tube is then cut and sealed off so that it fits inside the base.

Cathodes. Cathodes provide terminals for the arc and a source of electrons for lamp current.

34

In some lamps they function alternately as cathodes and anodes, but are commonly called cathodes. In other lamp designs, separate anodes are used because they best fit lamp design requirements. Plate anodes in high output lamps and wire anodes in *Power Groove* lamps are used to reduce the wattage loss at the lamp ends. Cathodes are usually made of coil-coiled, triple-coiled, or stick-coiled tungsten, like an ordinary lamp filament, except coils are filled with alkaline-earth oxides. These oxides emit electrons more freely, thus minimizing losses and keeping efficiency high.

Mercury Vapor. Droplets of liquid mercury are placed in the fluorescent tube during manufacture. During lamp operation, the mercury vaporizes to a very low pressure (about 1/100,000th of atmospheric pressure). At this pressure, the current through the vapor causes the vapor to radiate energy most strongly at one specific wavelength in the ultraviolet region, 253.7 nanometers. (A nanometer is one billionth of a meter). Higher mercury pressures tend to reduce the production of this ultraviolet line. The mercury pressure during operation is regulated by the temperature of the bulb wall.

Filling Gas. Besides mercury, the tube also contains a small quantity of a highly purified rare gas. Argon and argon-neon are most common, but sometimes krypton is used. The filling gases ionize readily when sufficient voltage is applied across the lamp. The ionized filling gas quickly decreases in resistance allowing current to flow and the mercury to vaporize.

Phosphor Coating. Transforms radiation into visible light. The fluorescent lamp gets its name from the fact that the phosphor coating fluoresces. The chemical make-up of the phosphor determines the color of the light produced. Phosphor particles in fluorescent coatings are extremely small—approximately 0.0007 inch in diameter. Careful control of phosphor particle size is necessary to obtain high lamp efficiency.

Fluorescence is defined as "the property of a material to become self-luminous when acted upon by radiant energy, such as ultraviolet or X-rays." This definition pinpoints the two elements required in a fluorescent lamp: 1. A source of radiant energy. 2. A material that fluoresces.

Many natural and synthetic materials exhibit fluorescence. In fluorescent lamps, a powder having this property is applied to the inner surface of the bulb, which is usually tubular in cross-section. The selection of the phosphors and certain additives, called "activators," determines the characteristics of the emitted radia-tion; that is, ultraviolet, colored light, or various shades of white light.

The source of radiant energy that acts on the fluorescent material is an electric arc which passes through mercury vapor within the tube. A lamp starts when the voltage between the cathodes is sufficient to strike an arc in the filling gas. As the current passes through the vapor, it causes changes in the energy levels of electrons in the individual mercury ions; energy is then released in the form of several wavelengths of visible and ultraviolet (invisible) energy. The latter is radiated to the tube wall, where it activates the fluorescent material and causes it to emit visible light.

The voltage needed to srike an arc through the length of the tube depends to a large extent on the temperature of the electron-emitting cathode. There are three types of starting arrangements.

The cathodes of the preheat lamp are preheated to emit electrons before the arc strikes; this is where the name "preheat" comes from. This type of lamp operation is also referred to as switch-start or starter-start. See circuits 1, 2 and 3.

The preheating process requires a few seconds. It is usually accomplished by an automatic starter which applies current to the cathodes of the lamp for sufficient time to heat them, and then automatically removes the current from the cathodes, causing the voltage to be applied between the cathodes and striking the arc. In some preheat systems, such as fluorescent desk lights, the preheating is accomplished by pushing a manual start button. This is held down for a few seconds. During this time, the cathodes heat. When the button is released, the arc strikes. Preheat lamps are usually identified by wattage, bulb diameter (in eighths of an inch), and color. Thus a lamp marked F15T8/CW is a 15-watt, 1-in. diameter, Cool White fluorescent lamp. With preheat lamps designed for appliance service, wattage varies widely depending on the ballast. These lamps are identified by length instead of wattage. For example, F26″ T8 for a lamp 26 inches long, 1-in. diameter.

Ballasts, also known as "choke coils," are available to operate certain preheat lamps without using starters. These ballasts use the rapid start principle of starting and operation. They are designed around the characteristics of the preheat lamps involved. These ballasts are popularly called "trigger start" ballasts.

To overcome the slow starting of the preheat system, General Electric introduced "instant start" lamps. In addition to lighting as soon as

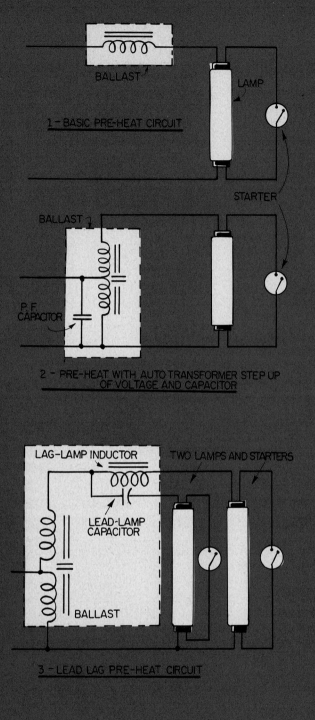

BALLAST

LAMP

1 - BASIC PRE-HEAT CIRCUIT

STARTER

BALLAST

P.F. CAPACITOR

2 - PRE-HEAT WITH AUTO TRANSFORMER STEP UP OF VOLTAGE AND CAPACITOR

LAG-LAMP INDUCTOR   TWO LAMPS AND STARTERS

LEAD-LAMP CAPACITOR

BALLAST

3 - LEAD LAG PRE-HEAT CIRCUIT

current to the lamp is turned on, instant start lamps also eliminate the need for starters, and thus simplify maintenance. See circuits 4, 5, 6.

Since slimline lamps can be operated at more than one current and wattage, they are identified by lamp length. The number following the F in the designation is the nominal lamp length in inches, rather than the lamp wattage as with most preheat lamps.

The "rapid start" is the most recent development in fluorescent types. Rapid start lamps start quickly without external starters such as required for the pre-heat type. Also, ballasts are smaller and more efficient. See circuits 7 and 8.

The new lamps utilize cathodes that can be heated continuously with very low losses. An incidental feature of the system is that it permits dimming and flashing, not possible with other types. Because of these multiple advantages, rapid start fixtures are used in most new lighting installations.

BALLASTS

The "ballast" required for all fluorescent lamp operation is essentially a single winding of wire on a laminated iron frame. It is sometimes In fluorescent circuits the ballast performs two independent functions. First, it momentarily increases the line voltage to overcome the high resistance between the widely separated cathodes, and establishes a conductive arc between them. The resistance of the path then becomes very low, so the ballast is left in the line to limit the current to a safe value. Without the ballast, the tube would draw so much current that it would destroy itself.

DIMMING

The light output of rapid start fluorescent lamps can be adjusted or dimmed by a number of special circuits. All of these incorporate one

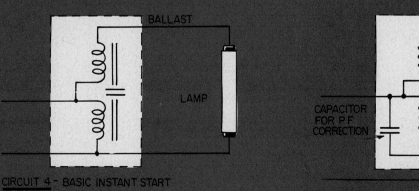

BALLAST

LAMP

CIRCUIT 4 - BASIC INSTANT START

BALLAST

CAPACITOR FOR P.F. CORRECTION

LAMP

CIRCUIT 5 - INSTANT START WITH DISCONNET LAMP HOLDER

essential principle: the ballast must keep the cathodes of the lamp energized at the proper voltage regardless of the amount the lamp is dimmed.

Current passing through the lamp or lamps in the dimming system can be controlled by a number of methods. These include thyratrons, silicon-controlled rectifiers and other solid-state devices, variable inductors, autotransformers, saturable core reactors, magnetic amplifiers, etc.

Dimming systems vary widely in performance. Some systems can dim lamps no lower than 20 percent of normal full output, while others can dim lamps as low as 0.2 percent.

FLASHING

The life of fluorescent lamps is seriously reduced by turning them on and off frequently when ordinary ballasts are used. However, it is possible to flash rapid start type lamps and maintain satisfactory life by using a special flashing ballast.

SPIRALING AND FLICKERING

Early in life, fluorescent lamps occasionally exhibit a condition called spiraling; i.e., the brightness varies from end to end. This condition is often caused by loose materials knocked off the cathode. Normally, it disappears after the lamps have been burned for a few hours.

UNDER AND OVERVOLTAGE

Ballasts are usually designed for operation on 120-volt circuits. In general, operation is satisfactory with voltage as low as 110 volts, or as high as 125 volts. Similarly, ballasts for 208-volt service operate satisfactorily from 200 to 215 volts; 240-volt service from 220 to 250 volts; 277-volt service from 250 to 290 volts; and 480-volt service from 440 to 500 volts.

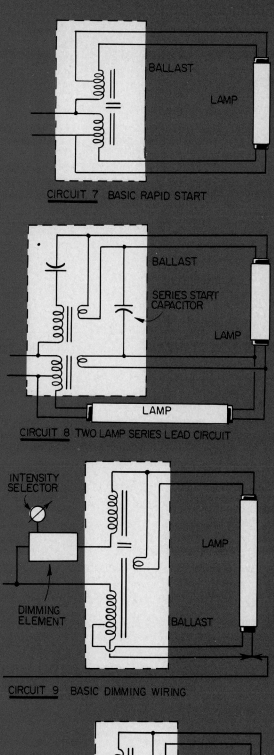

CIRCUIT 7 BASIC RAPID START

CIRCUIT 8 TWO LAMP SERIES LEAD CIRCUIT

CIRCUIT 9 BASIC DIMMING WIRING

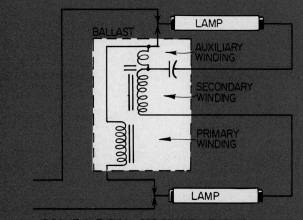

CIRCUIT 6 TYPICAL SERIES INSTANT START

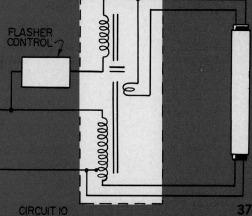

CIRCUIT 10

Trouble-Shooting Chart

STEPS IN FINDING TROUBLE

First find symptom here, noting the code number and letter. Then refer to that number and letter in the Sections below.

While the following symptoms apply particularly to preheat fluorescent lamps, most of the appearance factors also apply to the Instant Start, Slimline, Rapid Start, High Output, and Power Groove types as well.

NORMAL END OF LIFE
Lamp won't operate; or flashes momentarily and goes out; or blinks on and off, perhaps with shimmering effect; ends probably blackened. — **1-a.**

SHORT LIFE
— **1-f, 1-q, 2-a, 2-b, 3-a, 3-d, 3-g, 5-a, 6a, 6-c, 7-a.**

IMMEDIATE FAILURE OF NEW LAMPS
— **1-q, 3-d, 3-g, 6-c, 6-f.**

END BLACKENING
Dense blackening at one end or both, extending 2"-3" from base. — **1-b.**
Blackening, generally within 1" of ends. — **1-i.**
Blackening at one end only. — **6-a, 6-c, 1-l.**

Blackening early in life (indicates active material from electrodes being sputtered off too rapidly). — **1-q, 2-a, 2-b, 3-a, 5-a, 6-a, 6-c.**

RINGS
Brownish rings at one or both ends, about 2" from base. — **1-c.**

DENSE SPOTS
Black, about ½" wide, extending about half way around tube, centering about 1" from base. — **3-b.**

DARK STREAKS
Streaks lengthwise of tube. — **1-j.**

DARK SECTION OF TUBE
⅓ to ½ of tube gives no light (tubes longer than 24"). — **4b, 4-c, 6-e.**

ENDS ONLY LIGHTED
— **2-b, 6-b, 6-c.**

BLINKING ON AND OFF
Accompanied by shimmering effect during "lighted" period. — **1-a.**
Blinking of relatively new lamp. — **1-q, 1-k, 2-a, 3-a, 4-a, 4-c, 5-c, 6-a, 6-c.**

NO STARTING EFFORT, or SLOW STARTING
— **1-l. 1-m, 1-n, 1-p, 1-q, 2-c, 2-d, 3-a, 3-c, 3-e, 5-c, 6-c, 6-d.**

FLICKER (NOT STROBOSCOPIC EFFECT)
Pronounced, irregular flicker on looking directly at lamp (spiraling, swirling, snaking, etc). — **1-g, 2-e, 3-a, 5-b, 6-c.**
Flicker suddenly occurring — **1-h.**
Persistent tendency to flicker. — **1-k, 6-c.**

DECREASED LIGHT OUTPUT
— **4-b, 4-c, 4-d, 5-c, 6-c, 7-b,** (During first 100 hours' use — **1-d.**)

COLOR AND BRIGHTNESS DIFFERENCES
Different color appearance in different locations of same installation. — **1-e, 4-c, 7-c.**
Lamps operate at unequal brilliancy. — **4-c, 5-c, 6-c.**

NOISE
Humming sound, which may be steady, or may come and go. — **3-f, 3-j.**

OVERHEATED BALLAST
— **1-q, 3-d, 3-g, 3-h, 3-i, 5-d, 6-c, 6-f.**

RADIO INTERFERENCE
— **1-o, 6-g.**

1. LAMPS

	POSSIBLE CAUSES*	MAINTENANCE
1-a	Normal failure; active material on electrodes exhausted.	Replace lamp (remove old lamp promptly).
1-b	Normal — end of life.	Replace lamp.
1-c	May occur on some lamps during life.	Has no effect on lamp performance.
1-d	Light output during first 100 hours is above published rating, sometimes as much at 10%. (Rating is based on output at end of 100 hours.)	
1-e	Actual slight differences in lamps may be discernible; perhaps wrong color lamp used; possibly lamp outside limits of color standards; or apparent color difference may be only difference in brightness between old and new lamp.	Replace lamps if objectionable. (If warranted, color temperature can be checked in laboratory to determine whether there is a difference, and how much.)
1-f	Mortality laws (Lamps of shorter life are balanced out by those of longer life to give rated average life.)	
1-g	New lamp may flicker.	Flicker should clear up after lamp is operated or turned on and off a few times.
1-h	May suddenly develop in any lamp in normal service.	Should clear up if turned off for a few seconds.
1-i	Mercury deposit.	Should evaporate as lamp is operated.
1-j	Globules of mercury on lower (cooler) part.	Rotate tube 180°. Mercury may evaporate by increased warmth, though it may condense out again on cool side.
1-k	Possibly lamp at fault	Replace lamp. Investigate further if successive lamps blink or flicker in same lampholders.
1-l	Open circuit in electrodes, due to broken electrode, air leak, open weld, etc.	If open circuit is shown by test or inspection as in **3-e**, replace lamp.
1-m	Burned out electrode (might be caused by placing one end of lamp directly across 120 volts).	If open circuit is shown by test or inspection as in **3-e**, replace lamp.
1-n	Air leak in lamp. In test with test lamp (see **3-e**) leak is indicated by absence of fluorescent glow, though electrode lights up.	Replace lamp.
1-o	Lamp radiation "broadcasts" through radio receiver.	Locate aerial and radio at least 10 ft. from lamp; or shield aerial lead-in wire, provide good ground, and keep aerial proper out of lamp and line radiation range.
1-p	Dirt accumulation on 40-watt Rapid Start lamps may cause unreliable starting under high humidity conditions.	Cleaning lamps restores normal ease of starting.
1-q	Wrong lamp type used.	Replace with lamp type marked on ballast label.

for Fluorescent Lamps

2. STARTERS

	POSSIBLE CAUSES*	MAINTENANCE
2-a	Wrong type of starter or defective starter, causing on-off blink or prolonged flashing at each start.	Replace with proper starter. Watch Dog (automatic cutout) starters overcome on-off blinking or prolonged flashing.
2-b	Ends of lamp are lighted while rest of lamp is not; starter failure.	Replace starter.
2-c	Starter at end of life.	Replace Starter.
2-d	Starter sluggish.	Replace Starter.
2-e	Starter not performing properly to pre-heat electrodes.	Replace Starter.

3. AUXILIARIES & FIXTURES

	POSSIBLE CAUSES*	MAINTENANCE
3-a	Ballast installed not supplying specified electrical values.	Replace with ETL approved ballast of correct rating for lamp size.
3-b	May occur near end of life on some lamps, but if early in life, indicates excessive starting or operating current.	Check for ballast off-rating or unusually high circuit voltage.
3-c	Remote possibility of open-circuited ballast.	Check ballast.
3-d	Wrong type of ballast used (e.g., AC type on DC power, wrong voltage rating, instant-start ballast in rapid-start fixture, etc.).	Replace ballast with proper type.
3-e	Burned-out lamp electrodes due to: – broken lampholders. – grounding of combination lampholder and starting socket, mounted on metal. – one strand of conductor touching grounded fixture. – improper wiring. – D-C operation without necessary additional resistance. – ground from some other cause.	To determine necessity for replacing lamp, examine electrodes by viewing end of bulb against pinhole of light. (Or test by connecting base pins **in series** with test lamp† on 120-v circuit. Fluorescent glow means intact electrodes, and active electrons.) †Correct Various Test for F Lamp Size Lamps 60-w 14-w to 40-w. 25-w Small diameter or miniature. 200-w 90-w or 100-w
3-f	Slight transformer hum inherent in ballast equipment; varies in different ballasts. Objectionable amount may be due to improper installation or improper ballast design.	Tighten ballast bolts; where possible use 4 bolts instead of 2; tighten fixture louvers; glass side panels; wedge vibrating parts of fixture.
3-g	Short in ballast or capacitor.	Replace ballast or capacitor.
3-h	High ambient temperature inside fixture housing.	Refer to fixture manufacturer.
3-i	Prolonged blinking tends to heat ballast, and heating is aggravated under high ambient temperature inside fixture housing.	See "Blinking On and Off," under Behavior and correct the cause.
3-j	Overheated ballast.	See 3-g, 3-h, 3-i, 6-f.

4. TEMPERATURE

	POSSIBLE CAUSES*	MAINTENANCE
4-a	Low temperature (starting difficulty may be experienced below 50°F).	Use ballast and/or starter designed for minimum expected temperature.
4-b	Low temperature operation. (Below 65°F light loss may be 2% or more per degree F.)	Change to enclosed fixture properly designed for expected temperature range; or change to jacketed outdoor type lamp if available.
4-c	Cold drafts or winds hitting tube.	Enclose or protect lamp.
4-d	Where heat is confined around lamp, light loss is 1% per degree F.	Better ventilation of fixture.

5. VOLTAGE

	POSSIBLE CAUSES*	MAINTENANCE
5-a	Too low or too high voltage.	Check voltage with range on ballast nameplate.
5-b	High voltage starting.	Check voltage.
5-c	Low circuit voltage.	Check voltage and correct if possible.
5-d	High circuit voltage.	Check voltage and correct if possible.

6. CIRCUIT

	POSSIBLE CAUSES*	MAINTENANCE
6-a	Loose circuit contact (likely at lampholder).	Lampholders should be rigidly mounted; lamp securely seated.
6-b	In new installation, may be wiring or ground fault.	Check circuit wiring.
6-c	Ballast improperly or incompletely connected.	Study ballast label instructions and check connections.
6-d	Possible open circuit.	Test lamp in another circuit, being sure of proper contact in lampholders. Check voltage from one lampholder to the other. (Use voltmeter or 220-v, 100-w test lamp. Only one connection at each holder should be alive; hence 4 ways to check 2 live ones.) If no voltage indication from lampholders, check circuit leads to holders. If still no voltage, check circuit connection.
6-e	D-C operation without using reversing switches.	Install reversing switches.
6-f	Short in wiring.	Correct wiring.
6-g	Line radiation and line feedback. (Write for bulletin LS-121.)	Apply line filter at lamp or fixture; sometimes possible to apply filters at power outlet or panel box.

7. OPERATION

	POSSIBLE CAUSES*	MAINTENANCE
7-a	Too many lamp starts.	Average life dependent on number of starts and hours of operation.
7-b	Dust or dirt on lamp, fixture, walls, or ceiling.	Clean.
7-c	May be due to reflector finish, wall finish, other nearby light, room decorations, etc.	Interchange lamps before assuming color difference.

* Service problems may arise from a combination of causes — not always from one single cause.

Know Your Current Requirements

SOME PEOPLE blithely plug appliances into the wall outlets without regard for the capacity of the latter to handle the load. A particular branch circuit might be fused for 15 amperes, but this does not mean that each of the outlets on the line can provide 15 amperes independently of the others when all are being used. It means that the *total* current of 15 amps must not be exceeded. If you are making breakfast and turn on both a coffee pot (about five amps) and a toaster (about ten amps), almost anything else you plug in will probably pop the fuse or circuit breaker.

A little simple arithmetic can help you avoid brownouts. Study the accompanying chart and check off the appliances and machines in your own home. The figures here are for representative products, and are close enough for planning purposes. Of course, you should know what fuses protect what branch circuits, so you should be able to distribute the load to best advantage.

Note that the important figure in each case is the current in amperes that an appliance draws from the line. Fuses and breakers recognize only the current and not the actual working power in watts.

If you plan to install any new current consuming equipment your utility will be only too happy to advise you if you have adequate power and if not, how large a service you will need.

Know the wattage of your appliance or tool and the size of the circuit wire before you plug in. Its safer for the house and the equipment.

Small-Current Class, to 5 amps,
120 volts (600 watts)

Razor—1/10 amp (10-15 watts).
All incandescent lamps—½ amp per 60 watts.
All fluorescent lamps—½ amp per 40 watts.
Fan, 10-inch size—1 amp (75 watts).
Solid-state radio set—1/10 amp (7 watts).
Tube-type radio set—1 amp (75 watts).
Hi-Fi record player—2 amps (150 watts).
Food mixer—2½ amps (200 watts).
Refrigerator—3 amps (250 watts).
Television set—4 amps (300 watts).
Vacuum cleaner—5 amps (400 watts).
Coffee pot—5 amps (600 watts).

Medium-Current Class, to 15 amps,
120 volts (1800 watts)

Portable heater—7 amps (840 watts).
Hand iron—9 amps (1000 watts).
Toaster—9½ amps (1100 watts).
Rotisserie—12 to 13 amps (1400-1500 watts).
Window air-conditioner—6 to 15 amps (600-1500 watts).
Clothes washer—12 amps (1500 watts).
Dishwasher—13 amps (1650 watts).
Mangle—15 amps (1650 watts).

Heavy Current Class, to 50 amps,
120/240 volts (12,000 watts)

Water heater—11 amps (2500 watts).
Window air-conditioner—15 amps (3000 watts).
Clothes dryer—25 amps (5600 watts).
Central air-conditioner—30 amps (6000 watts).
Range—30 to 60 amps (8000-16,000 watts).

Home Workshop Tools, to 15 amps,
120 volts (1800 watts)

Portable drill—1½ amps (200 watts).
Saber saw—3½ amps (400 watts).
Drill press—8 amps (800 watts).
Portable saw—9 amps (1200 watts).
Bench saw—14 amps (1680 watts).

AMPERE CAPACITY OF WIRE

COPPER		ALUMINUM	
SIZE	AMPERES	SIZE	AMPERES
14	15	12	15
12	20	10	25
10	30	8	30
8	40	6	40
ENTRANCE		ENTRANCE	
4	100	2	100
1	150	2/0	150
2/0	200	4/0	200

The above table indicates the allowable ampacity of branch and entrance lines of insulated copper and insulated aluminum and copper-clad aluminum conductors. It is intended for reference purposes only. Please consult Article 310 titled "Conductors for General Wiring" in the National Electrical Code for One and Two Family Dwellings. See page 123.

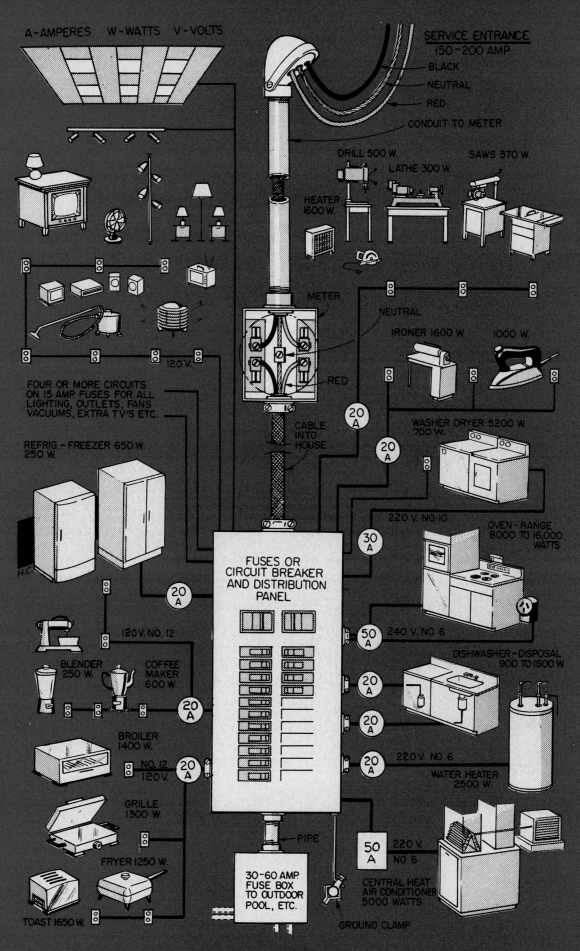

A - AMPERES   W - WATTS   V - VOLTS

SERVICE ENTRANCE
150 - 200 AMP.

BLACK
NEUTRAL
RED
CONDUIT TO METER

DRILL 500 W.   SAWS 570 W.
LATHE 300 W.
HEATER
1600 W.

METER

NEUTRAL

IRONER 1600 W.   1000 W.

RED

20 A

FOUR OR MORE CIRCUITS
ON 15 AMP. FUSES FOR ALL
LIGHTING, OUTLETS, FANS
VACUUMS, EXTRA TV'S ETC.

CABLE
INTO
HOUSE

20 A

WASHER DRYER 5200 W.
700 W.

REFRIG. - FREEZER 650 W.
250 W.

220 V. NO. 10

30 A

OVEN - RANGE
8000 TO 16,000
WATTS

H.C.

FUSES OR
CIRCUIT BREAKER
AND DISTRIBUTION
PANEL

20 A

50 A   240 V. NO. 6

120 V. NO. 12

DISHWASHER - DISPOSAL
900 TO 1800 W.

BLENDER   COFFEE
250 W.   MAKER
          600 W.

20 A

20 A

BROILER
1400 W.

NO. 12
120 V.

20 A

20 A   220 V. NO. 6

WATER HEATER
2500 W.

GRILLE
1300 W.

PIPE

50 A   220 V.

FRYER 1250 W.

30-60 AMP.
FUSE BOX
TO OUTDOOR
POOL, ETC.

NO. 6
CENTRAL HEAT
AIR CONDITIONER
5000 WATTS.

TOAST 1650 W.

GROUND CLAMP

Upgrading Your Service

If you are one of the millions of homes with an entrance service of 60 amperes or less, you just can't take advantage of the new appliances.

Electric ranges, hot water and space heaters require tremendous power. This new Tappan ceramic cooktop is rated at 13,000 watts and is much easier to clean than conventional surface units.

YOU FIND a 15-year-old house that appeals to you and your family because it offers plenty of living space, is in good condition, and is for sale at an attractive price. In checking it from roof to basement, you learn that it has three-wire, 240-volt electric service, fused at 60 amperes. After quickly adding up the probable current requirements of the new appliances you expect to buy, you realize that 60 amperes would scarcely take care of a water heater and a kitchen range.

"Guess we'll have to get the power company to run in a bigger line," you say to your wife. Power companies are happy to sell you all the juice you want, providing the transformer feeding the house is big enough to stand a little extra load. If there is a general demand for more current in the area, the utility will put in a bigger transformer, providing the generating station has some reserve capacity. It will run a new and heavier line to your house, to a new and bigger meter, *but at this point it stops.* From the house side of the meter (or from the house side of the main switch) the upgrading of the house circuits is *your* responsibility.

Obviously, there's not much advantage in having a 150-amp service (a highly recommended level) connected to wiring that was planned originally for a limited number of 15- and 20-ampere outlets.

CAN YOU DO IT YOURSELF?

If the house is enough of a bargain, there is no reason why you cannot do your own electrical upgrading. Thousands of Americans have done their own house wiring and upgrading and there is no reason in the world why you cannot do likewise. Some communities insist that a licensed electrician examine the work after you are done to make sure it meets the local code; others send over their own inspector to examine the work—and still others will actually give you a handbook describing how the work should be done.

The professional electrician has the experience and can do it faster than you can, but, if you are the least bit handy with tools, you can do just as good a job as he can—only it will take you longer. Incidentally, the large mail-order houses will even loan you the tools required to do your own wiring—and their clientele is vast!

The existing fuse or circuit-breaker box doesn't necessarily have to be replaced, as it can continue to protect the 15-amp lines that will be retained. However, for a little extra cost you can buy a new box, containing only breakers, that will be more convenient for any member of the family to use in case of an appliance failure that causes a short-circuit, or an overload. While you are at it, replace all two-hole outlets with the three-hole grounding type outlet and add a GFI (ground fault interrupter) in the laundry area and possibly in the garage.

All this sounds like a lot of work, and it is, but when it's finished you'll have an electrical system on which you can depend. If you are handy with tools and are willing to spend some spare time you can do a first-class job, and you'll save plenty doing it yourself.

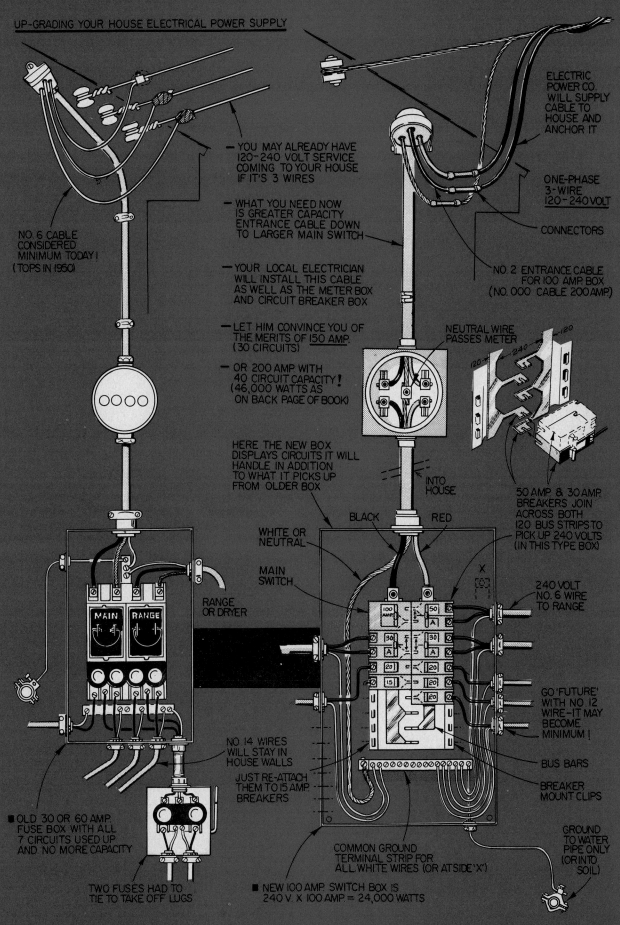

UP-GRADING YOUR HOUSE ELECTRICAL POWER SUPPLY

NO. 6 CABLE CONSIDERED MINIMUM TODAY! (TOPS IN 1950)

— YOU MAY ALREADY HAVE 120-240 VOLT SERVICE COMING TO YOUR HOUSE IF IT'S 3 WIRES

— WHAT YOU NEED NOW IS GREATER CAPACITY ENTRANCE CABLE DOWN TO LARGER MAIN SWITCH

— YOUR LOCAL ELECTRICIAN WILL INSTALL THIS CABLE AS WELL AS THE METER BOX AND CIRCUIT BREAKER BOX

— LET HIM CONVINCE YOU OF THE MERITS OF 150 AMP. (30 CIRCUITS)

— OR 200 AMP. WITH 40 CIRCUIT CAPACITY! (46,000 WATTS AS ON BACK PAGE OF BOOK)

HERE THE NEW BOX DISPLAYS CIRCUITS IT WILL HANDLE IN ADDITION TO WHAT IT PICKS UP FROM OLDER BOX

ELECTRIC POWER CO. WILL SUPPLY CABLE TO HOUSE AND ANCHOR IT

ONE-PHASE 3-WIRE 120-240 VOLT CONNECTORS

NO. 2 ENTRANCE CABLE FOR 100 AMP BOX (NO. 000 CABLE 200AMP)

NEUTRAL WIRE PASSES METER

INTO HOUSE

BLACK   RED

WHITE OR NEUTRAL

MAIN SWITCH

RANGE OR DRYER

MAIN   RANGE

NO. 14 WIRES WILL STAY IN HOUSE WALLS

JUST RE-ATTACH THEM TO 15 AMP. BREAKERS

■ OLD 30 OR 60 AMP. FUSE BOX WITH ALL 7 CIRCUITS USED UP AND NO MORE CAPACITY

TWO FUSES HAD TO TIE TO TAKE OFF LUGS

COMMON GROUND TERMINAL STRIP FOR ALL WHITE WIRES (OR AT SIDE 'X')

■ NEW 100 AMP. SWITCH BOX IS 240 V. X 100 AMP. = 24,000 WATTS

50 AMP. & 30 AMP. BREAKERS JOIN ACROSS BOTH 120 BUS STRIPS TO PICK UP 240 VOLTS (IN THIS TYPE BOX)

240 VOLT NO. 6 WIRE TO RANGE

GO 'FUTURE' WITH NO. 12 WIRE—IT MAY BECOME MINIMUM !

BUS BARS

BREAKER MOUNT CLIPS

GROUND TO WATER PIPE ONLY (OR INTO SOIL)

Wiring You Can Do

Electrical work requires some knowledge, confidence in yourself, the right tools and supplies. Here is some information that will help.

THE EXPRESSION "new work" can mean two things: 1, Wiring, outlets, switches, protective devices, etc., in a house under construction. Or, 2, Additional facilities in a completed house already occupied by the owner.

If you are having a house custom-built, your architect will take care of the details of the electrical system in the blueprints that he will turn over to the building contractor. Obviously, you and the architect must get together during the early stages of the planning and decide what you want or should have. For instance, you might think that a 100-ampere service is enough for your anticipated needs, but he will probably recommend 150 because the labor cost is the same and the materials only cost a little more. Once you approve the overall plans for the house, don't make changes unless you are prepared to pay heavily for them.

Most new houses built during the 1970's have very good electrical systems because builders have learned that this feature is a strong selling point. A typical three-bedroom house of the 1950's had two-wire, 30-ampere service, whereas its later counterpart is more likely to have three-wire, 60- or 100-ampere.

After you've lived in a place for a year or so you may well decide that you want to add a finished playroom or den in the basement, a patio off the kitchen, or some similar improvement. If you can handle the carpentry and masonry work that these projects entail, you can certainly do the extra electrical wiring.

A basement project is the easiest of all because in the vast majority of such houses the circuit breaker or fuse box is in open sight on the wall through which the service wires from the utility company enter. In most breaker boxes there are spare positions into which breakers for the new circuits can be inserted. If

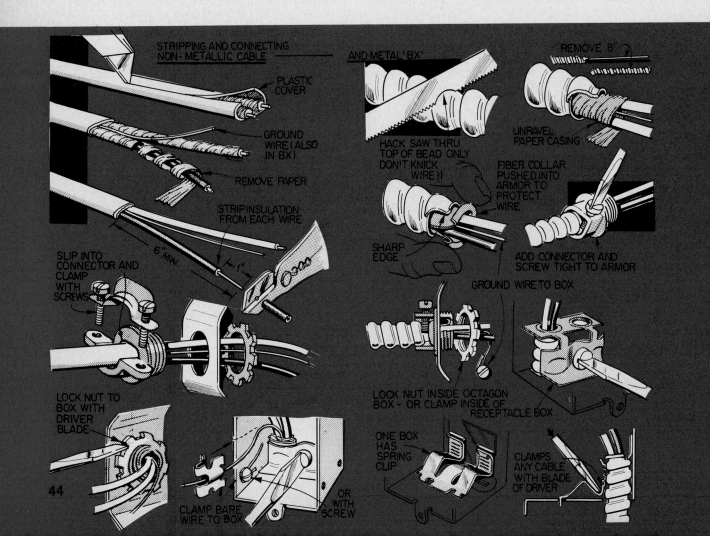

there are no spares (or if all the fuse positions are filled) simply mount a new, small breaker box next to the existing box. To connect this to the main line, just after the main switch or main fuse, you must of course deactivate the line. This means that the whole house goes dead while you fasten the two or three wires from the new box, so warn your family in advance, have a flashlight handy, and don't forget to reset electric clocks, thermostat shut-offs, and other automatic timing controls.

There is nothing wrong about mixing an existing fuse box with a new circuit-breaker box. They both react the same way to overloads of current.

If you are buying in a "development project" you can order additional wiring and outlets (at extra cost, of course) if the house hasn't been started at all, or if it is in the form of a hollow shell.

TYPES OF WIRING

Plastic Sheathed, or Romex also known as Non-Metallic: This consists of two or three insulated wires, with or without a bare grounding wire, enclosed in a durable molded insulating material. The better grades are thoroughly weatherproof and can even be buried in the ground for circuits to outdoor lights. Two-wire cable is flat; three-wire is round.

Plastic sheathed is far and away the most widely used cable for house wiring. It is relatively inexpensive and easy to mount and connect.

Flexible Armored Cable, also known as BX: Contains two or three insulated wires, usually with a bare grounding wire. The latter supplements the grounding function of the spiral, galvanized steel cover. The steel cover is not waterproof, so the cable is suitable only for indoor use.

Conduit: This is merely empty piping, made in two weights: rigid and thin-wall. As you might guess, the first is stronger than the second. The standard length is 10 feet. Numerous couplings, bushings, straps and other fittings are available for mounting and connecting to electrical fixtures.

The empty conduit is mounted first and the wires pulled through them afterward. If the pipes are fairly short and don't have too many right-angle elbows, the usual No. 14 and No. 12 wires can be pushed through. For longer runs a long, flexible steel tape called a "snake" is needed. This is started at one outlet or switch box and wiggled until it reappears at the next

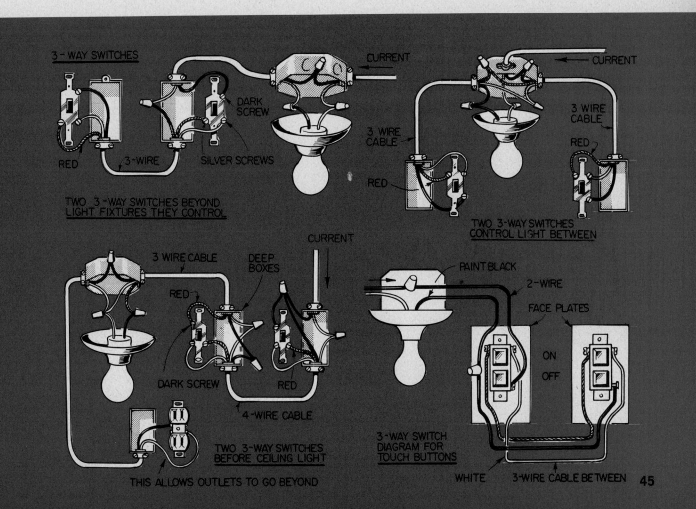

3 - WAY SWITCHES

TWO 3 - WAY SWITCHES BEYOND LIGHT FIXTURES THEY CONTROL

TWO 3-WAY SWITCHES CONTROL LIGHT BETWEEN

TWO 3-WAY SWITCHES BEFORE CEILING LIGHT

THIS ALLOWS OUTLETS TO GO BEYOND

3-WAY SWITCH DIAGRAM FOR TOUCH BUTTONS

WHITE   3-WIRE CABLE BETWEEN   45

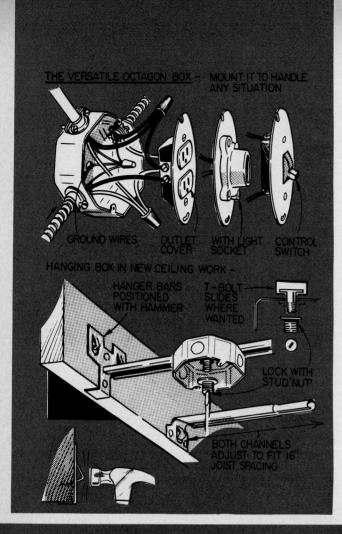

THE VERSATILE OCTAGON BOX – MOUNT IT TO HANDLE ANY SITUATION

GROUND WIRES   OUTLET COVER   WITH LIGHT SOCKET   CONTROL SWITCH

HANGING BOX IN NEW CEILING WORK –

HANGER BARS POSITIONED WITH HAMMER

T-BOLT SLIDES WHERE WANTED

LOCK WITH STUD NUT

BOTH CHANNELS ADJUST TO FIT 16" JOIST SPACING

open box. One wire at a time is twisted around a loop at the end of the snake and fished through. The process is tedious and uncertain, and often very frustrating because the wires tend to snag at 90° turns. For difficult bends special grease is available to make the pull easier. With thin-wall conduit this problem is alleviated to a great extent because the pipe can be bent into a smooth quarter-circle turn about a foot in radius by means of a tool called a conduit bender. Rigid conduit lives up to its name; it doesn't bend, and it must be handled just like piping for water or gas.

While plastic-sheathed and armored cable can be bought almost anywhere, conduit is generally available from electrical supply firms that sell mostly to contractors and from the large mail order firms. It is virtually unknown in parts of the country where it is not required by local codes.

After you've done some basement wiring you might get ambitious and decide to tackle other parts of the house. Consider all the factors involved.

Is the house of the ranch type, with a single large living area above the cellar? Is the

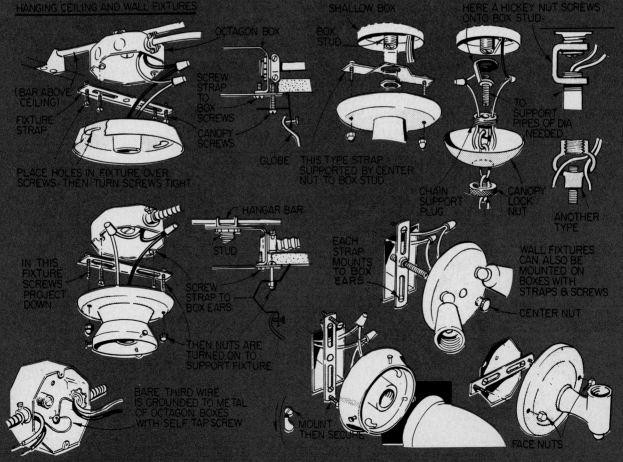

HANGING CEILING AND WALL FIXTURES

OCTAGON BOX

(BAR ABOVE CEILING)
FIXTURE STRAP

SCREW STRAP TO BOX SCREWS

CANOPY SCREWS

PLACE HOLES IN FIXTURE OVER SCREWS - THEN TURN SCREWS TIGHT

GLOBE   THIS TYPE STRAP SUPPORTED BY CENTER NUT TO BOX STUD

SHALLOW BOX

BOX STUD

HERE A HICKEY NUT SCREWS ONTO BOX STUD

TO SUPPORT PIPES OF DIA NEEDED

CHAIN SUPPORT PLUG

CANOPY LOCK NUT

ANOTHER TYPE

IN THIS FIXTURE SCREWS PROJECT DOWN

HANGAR BAR

STUD

SCREW STRAP TO BOX EARS

THEN NUTS ARE TURNED ON TO SUPPORT FIXTURE

EACH STRAP MOUNTS TO BOX EARS

WALL FIXTURES CAN ALSO BE MOUNTED ON BOXES WITH STRAPS & SCREWS

CENTER NUT

BARE THIRD WIRE IS GROUNDED TO METAL OF OCTAGON BOXES WITH SELF TAP SCREW

MOUNT THEN SECURE

FACE NUTS

basement's ceiling fully open, allowing access to the floor of the living area? Or did you strain your neck putting up a beautiful ceiling of sound-absorbing tiles, thus preventing you from boring holes in the ceiling? Is the house of the two-story variety, with the living room, dining room and kitchen on the first level and two or three bedrooms and one or two bathrooms on the top?

A common form of new work is running an individual line from a circuit breaker or fuse to a new outlet near a window of the living room or a bedroom, to power an air-conditioner and to remove this load from an existing outlet that is sharing a breaker or fuse with five or six other outlets. In a ranch house with an open cellar ceiling, the main part of the job is probing for the space between cellar beams under the window by means of a long, thin twist drill in a hand or power drill, at the point where the floor of the room meets the wall. Cellar beams are usually two or three inches thick and 16 inches apart on centers, so it doesn't take more than a couple of exploratory holes to find a spot where you can go through with a larger bit for the plastic or armored cable. The latter won't even

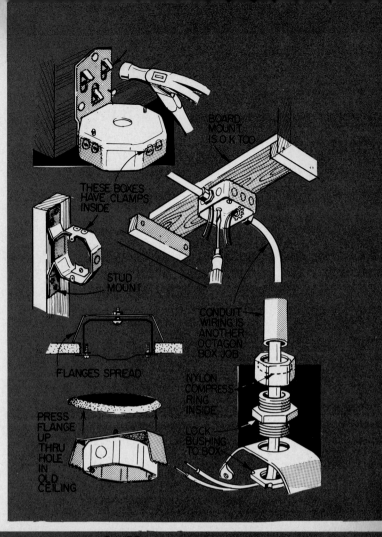

THESE BOXES HAVE CLAMPS INSIDE

BOARD MOUNT IS O.K TOO

STUD MOUNT

CONDUIT WIRING IS ANOTHER OCTAGON BOX JOB

FLANGES SPREAD

NYLON COMPRESS-RING INSIDE

PRESS FLANGE UP THRU HOLE IN OLD CEILING

LOCK BUSHING TO BOX

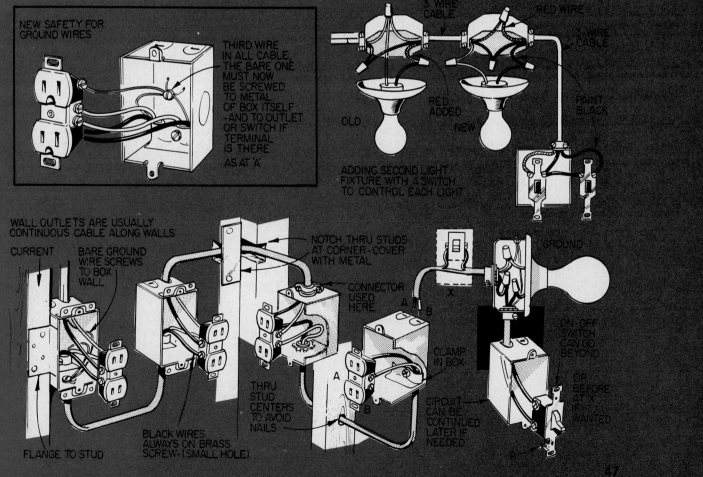

NEW SAFETY FOR GROUND WIRES

THIRD WIRE IN ALL CABLE, THE BARE ONE MUST NOW BE SCREWED TO METAL OF BOX ITSELF - AND TO OUTLET OR SWITCH IF TERMINAL IS THERE AS AT 'A'

3-WIRE CABLE

RED WIRE

3-WIRE CABLE

OLD

RED ADDED

NEW

PAINT BLACK

ADDING SECOND LIGHT FIXTURE WITH A SWITCH TO CONTROL EACH LIGHT

WALL OUTLETS ARE USUALLY CONTINUOUS CABLE ALONG WALLS

CURRENT

BARE GROUND WIRE SCREWS TO BOX WALL

NOTCH THRU STUDS AT CORNER-COVER WITH METAL

CONNECTOR USED HERE

GROUND

X

A B

CLAMP IN BOX

ON-OFF SWITCH CAN GO BEYOND

THRU STUD CENTERS TO AVOID NAILS

A

B

A

CIRCUIT CAN BE CONTINUED LATER IF NEEDED

OR BEFORE AT X IF WANTED

FLANGE TO STUD

BLACK WIRES ALWAYS ON BRASS SCREW- (SMALL HOLE)

A

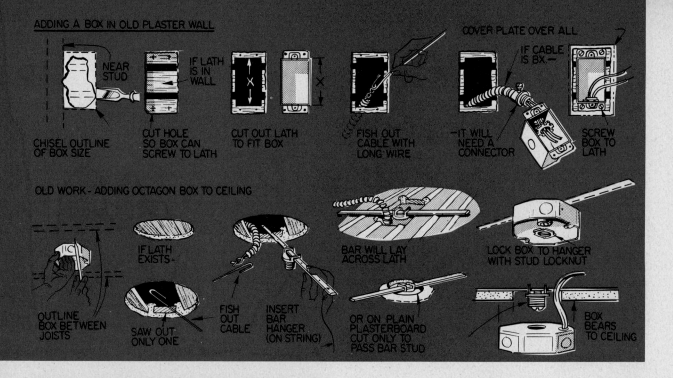

ADDING A BOX IN OLD PLASTER WALL

CHISEL OUTLINE OF BOX SIZE — NEAR STUD

CUT HOLE SO BOX CAN SCREW TO LATH — IF LATH IS IN WALL

CUT OUT LATH TO FIT BOX

FISH OUT CABLE WITH LONG WIRE

—IT WILL NEED A CONNECTOR

COVER PLATE OVER ALL — IF CABLE IS BX.—

SCREW BOX TO LATH

OLD WORK - ADDING OCTAGON BOX TO CEILING

OUTLINE BOX BETWEEN JOISTS

IF LATH EXISTS-

SAW OUT ONLY ONE

FISH OUT CABLE

INSERT BAR HANGER (ON STRING)

BAR WILL LAY ACROSS LATH

OR ON PLAIN PLASTERBOARD CUT ONLY TO PASS BAR STUD

LOCK BOX TO HANGER WITH STUD LOCKNUT

BOX BEARS TO CEILING

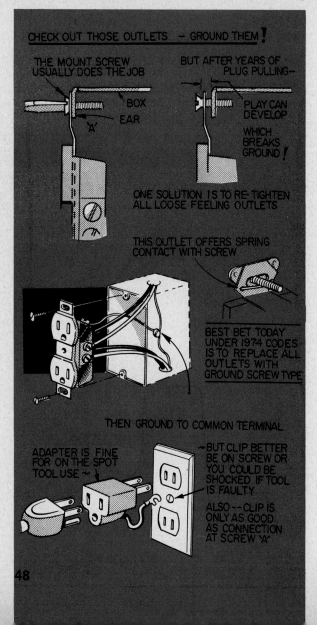

CHECK OUT THOSE OUTLETS — GROUND THEM!

THE MOUNT SCREW USUALLY DOES THE JOB

BOX
EAR
"A"

BUT AFTER YEARS OF PLUG PULLING-

PLAY CAN DEVELOP WHICH BREAKS GROUND!

ONE SOLUTION IS TO RE-TIGHTEN ALL LOOSE FEELING OUTLETS

THIS OUTLET OFFERS SPRING CONTACT WITH SCREW

BEST BET TODAY UNDER 1974 CODES IS TO REPLACE ALL OUTLETS WITH GROUND SCREW TYPE

THEN GROUND TO COMMON TERMINAL

ADAPTER IS FINE FOR ON THE SPOT TOOL USE -

→BUT CLIP BETTER BE ON SCREW OR YOU COULD BE SHOCKED IF TOOL IS FAULTY

ALSO -- CLIP IS ONLY AS GOOD AS CONNECTION AT SCREW 'A'

be visible if you terminate it at an outlet of the "surface mounting" type, fastened to the wall at the floor line.

The same technique can also be used in bringing a television antenna lead-in, and the control wires of a directional rotator if the antenna is so equipped, to the TV set. From the roof, route these through a basement window frame, along the ceiling beams, and up to the floor line of the TV room.

SECOND STORY WORK

Suppose that you want to put the air-conditioner on the second floor. The trick now is to probe for holes at the corners where the walls of the first-floor room meet at the ceiling, and likewise, where the corresponding walls of the second-floor room meet at the floor line. If these holes are fairly well lined up, tack a length of three-wire plastic cable into the corner of the room. Paint it as well as you can to match the room color. It won't be invisible, but neither will it be too conspicuous. It more than justifies intrusion into the room if it enables the air-conditioner to cool efficiently without popping the circuit breaker or fuse.

Oddly enough, many people overlook entirely the possibility of running a much-needed second-story line on the *outside* of a house. Outdoor type plastic-covered cable is ideal for the purpose; it lies flat, can be secured firmly with staples, and can be painted. The idea is to start the new line at the breaker box and to take it outdoors through a hole in the frame of a basement window. Upstairs, bring it indoors through another hole, in the bedroom window if the frame is of wood or in the wall if it is metal, and terminate it in a surface-mounted outlet.

THE BASEMENTLESS HOUSE

Thousands of homes in the United States do not have basements at all, but sit merely on slabs of concrete. The power line from the local utility goes through the meter and the main switch, on the outside of the house, and then into the attic. At a point above the kitchen or the laundry room it drops through a wall to a circuit breaker or fuse box. From here the branch circuits to the other parts of the house, go up through a wall to the attic, and down from the attic through walls to the various rooms. There is not much flexibility to this arrangement, because the attic is generally low and has very little crawl space.

If you want to install an outlet on an outside wall, for lights and a TV set on a patio, look for an inside outlet under or near a window facing the outdoor area and determine if it is practical to drill a hole through the back of the outlet box and through the wall.

If you plan to use an electric grille on the patio, to avoid the smoke and danger of a charcoal fire, you'll need a separate 15- or 20-ampere line from the breaker box, as grilles take a lot of juice. Emerging from the box, this might be run on the ceiling of the laundry room, through the outer wall to the eaves, along the eaves and from there to a convenient wall position for the outlet. It will hardly be noticeable.

LIGHTING THE ATTIC

If the attic of a ranch-type or two-story house is readily accessible and has head space in it, you might use it for dead storage. As you need light there for only short periods, you can get by safely with a well-insulated three-wire extension cord, plugged into a wall outlet of a bedroom. The other end can be snaked through holes in the side and the ceiling of a clothes closet and into the attic near the opening for the ladder or stairs from below.

If the attic has a window and you plan to put an exhaust fan in it (a very good idea!), you will want a permanent line. An outside one from the basement or laundry room is probably the easiest to install.

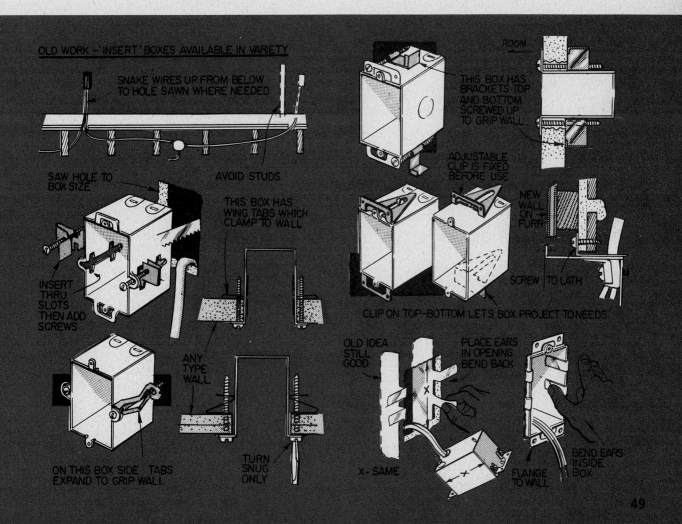

Electrical Plumbing

THE INSTALLATION, repair and replacement of certain electrically-operated machines is more in the plumbing field than in the electrical. In this category are dishwashers, disposals, water heaters, gas-heated clothes dryers, pumps, lawn sprinklers with timer switches, and swimming pool pumps. To do any serious work on these you may need some special tools.

SPECIAL PRECAUTIONS

All electrical devices connected in any way to water or gas pipes must be given extra-special attention because the latter are always part of the "grounded" side of all power lines. Any defect or breakdown in the insulation that separates this grounded side from the "hot" ungrounded side is likely to make the metal frame or case of an appliance "hot" in relation to any other grounded objects such as faucets, sinks, stoves, radiators, and even wet floors and damp grass. This is a very dangerous condition, and is the cause of many shocking accidents.

Water lines are ideal "grounds" because they consist of miles of iron, copper or brass pipes buried in the earth. Even the comparatively short piping from individual house wells is a good ground.

To assure electrical continuity of the pipe systems in houses, most building codes require heavy wire jumpers between the inlet and outlet fittings of water meters, even though the latter generally are made of cast brass.

OPEN THE CIRCUIT

Before doing any minor repair or maintenance on "wet" machines, be sure to *remove* the fuse or open the circuit breaker in the electrical circuit and to *close* the nearest water shutoff. Have a bucket or a large pan on hand, to catch the water that drains out of pipes above the level of the fixture being opened.

When you have to do something on a water heater you'll learn that there is a shut-off valve in the cold-water line but none in the hot. How do you turn off the hot? Easily, by turning off the cold water! The hot water leaves the tank only because it is pushed by the incoming cold, so only one shut-off is needed.

The circulation pumps of hot water heating systems require little maintenance. Some bearings do not require oil but those that do are fitted with a oil cap and tube that leads to the bearing.

Incidentally, removal of a worn-out heater and installation of a new one is a job within the resources of most home owners, and usually requires only a wrench and lots of muscle. The wrench is for undoing the pipe fittings, and the muscle is for disposing of the water in the tank itself. If the heater is in a basement and the nearest (and possibly the only) drain is a laundry tub on the same level, you will have to use the bucket-and-dump method. Forty gallons of water weigh 334 pounds, so take it easy and do the job in installments. If the heater is in a utility room near the kitchen above ground level, or in an attached garage, hook-up a length of garden hose to the drain cock and let the water empty into the garden. It will do some good there.

If the spacing of the pipe fittings on the new heater is not quite the same as on the old one, you may have to use shorter or longer connections. Pre-threaded pieces of short pipe are called "nipples" and are available in lengths from one to 12 inches. Many hardware and do-it-yourself stores cut and thread pipe to order, often while you wait.

Connections That Stay Put

IN ELECTRICAL WORK one of the most frequent jobs is joining wires or fastening wires to terminals on switches, sockets, outlets, and plugs. A good joint, or connection, is one that is clean and tight. If it is dirty and loose it can heat up and under some circumstances it can cause serious fire damage.

All splices and joints of circuit line should be made in a separate junction box if more than four connections are necessary. Otherwise a deep gem or hex box can be used.

MAKING A JOINT

After removing the outer insulation, clean the wire with a strip of emery cloth or the back of a knife. The quickest and simplest joint, (see drawing) is made by twisting the bare ends together and soldering them with rosin-core solder. Leave the tip of the iron against the wires for at least three or four seconds to cook out excess rosin. Wipe the joint with a clean rag and cover with two layers of plastic electrical tape.

WIRE NUTS

Soldering is unnecessary if the wires are snugly clamped by insulated "solderless connectors," as shown. These look like the caps of toothpaste tubes, are threaded on the inside, and simply screw over the bare wires. These wire nuts are easy to remove when wiring must be changed and they are the only practical means of joining aluminum wire. To lengthen flexible cord, make staggered joints as shown.

The trick in attaching wires to screw terminals is to form a hook-shaped loop and to squeeze this under the screw, without overlap, before tightening the latter. The loop should be made in a *clockwise* direction so that it will not be loosened when the screw is tightened.

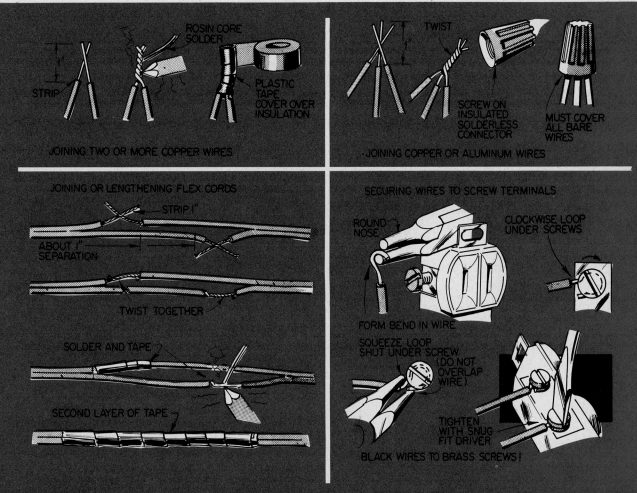

JOINING TWO OR MORE COPPER WIRES

STRIP — ROSIN CORE SOLDER — PLASTIC TAPE COVER OVER INSULATION

JOINING COPPER OR ALUMINUM WIRES

TWIST — SCREW ON INSULATED SOLDERLESS CONNECTOR — MUST COVER ALL BARE WIRES

JOINING OR LENGTHENING FLEX CORDS

STRIP 1" — ABOUT 1" SEPARATION — TWIST TOGETHER — SOLDER AND TAPE — SECOND LAYER OF TAPE

SECURING WIRES TO SCREW TERMINALS

ROUND NOSE — CLOCKWISE LOOP UNDER SCREWS — FORM BEND IN WIRE — SQUEEZE LOOP SHUT UNDER SCREW (DO NOT OVERLAP WIRE) — TIGHTEN WITH SNUG FIT DRIVER — BLACK WIRES TO BRASS SCREWS!

Installing Outlets and Switches

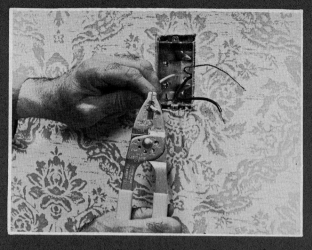

Strip away an inch of insulation from each wire. Note that one wire is black, other is white. Connect white wire to nickle-plated terminal and black wire to brass-plated terminal. This is important.

There is no need to call in an electrician to replace a faulty switch. It's an easy job, even for a woman.

THE FIRST STEP is to flip off the circuit breaker or remove the fuse that controls the circuit to the switch. Next, remove the cover plate by unscrewing its two screws. This will expose the switch. Remove the top and bottom screws that hold the switch in the box. Now, gently pull out the switch to expose the two screws that connect the wires to the switch. Note that one wire is black (or red) and the second wire is white. Normally, the white wire is the ground wire, but if it is used as a "hot" line, it should be painted black at the end. This is a legal requirement as all "hot" wires must be black or painted black. Loosen the two screws holding the wires in place so you can remove the switch. Do not tamper with any other wires you may find in the box except those connected to the switch. These wires may feed other lights or outlets and have nothing to do with the switch.

When you install the new switch connect it the same way as the old one. Make sure the switch will be in the off position when the toggle is down. If you replace the switch with a silent mercury-type switch, look for the word Top stamped on the switch body and install with this word on top. When you make the wire connections, wrap the wires around the screws in a clockwise direction so that tightening the screws will keep the wires wrapped around the shank of the screws.

THREE-WAY SWITCHES

Three-way switches are used to control the same light from two different locations. Replacement of these switches is the same as for conventional switches except they have three connections instead of two—usually one wire at the top of the switch and two at the bottom. Mark the wires so you will know to which screw they go before removing them. If the replacement is a mercury-type switch, install it with the word Top at the top. Unlike conventional switches, the toggle position on a three-way switches does not necessarily mean the light is on when the toggle is up, or off when the toggle is down. The On and Off positions of either switch depend upon the On or Off positions of the other switch.

INSTALLING A NEW SWITCH

YOU CAN CONTROL an overhead ceiling light operated by a pull chain by connecting it to a wall switch. First turn off the current going to the ceiling light by removing the fuse or flipping the circuit breaker to Off. Next, determine where you want the switch located. A wall switch should always be on the door knob side of the wall, about four feet from the floor. Tap the wall to locate the studs, or drill a series of 1/16-inch holes to find the stud. Trace the outline of the metal box that will house the switch on the wall so that one side will be next to the stud. Drill a hole in each corner and use a keyhole saw to cut away the plaster.

Next you will have to pass a cable (BX or plastic) long enough to reach from the light to the switch position. To do this you will need a brace, a long bit, and an electrician's snake. Drill the holes as shown in the drawing to pass the cable. Fish for the cable with the snake. Insert one end of the cable through one of the knockouts in the ceiling box after removing about five inches of the outer protective coating to expose the two insulated wires. Strip off an inch of insulation from each wire. Disconnect the black wire to the ceiling light and connect it to the black wire of the new cable. The white wire of the new cable goes to the black wire that was formerly connected to the ceiling light. Solder and tape the connections or use wire nuts. Note that the white wire from the fuse box to the ceiling light is not disturbed.

Now go back to the opening in the wall for the switch. Push the cable back into the opening and try the switch box for fit. The box should rest against the side of the wall stud. Remove the box and drill two holes in the side of the box for mounting. Make the pilot holes for the screws with an awl bent to a right angle. Pass the cable through one of the knockouts and clamp it in place after first removing about five inches of the outer protective covering. Strip off about an inch of insulation from each wire. Now push the box back into the opening and secure it to the wall with two round-head Phillips screws and an offset screwdriver. Where a stud is not in position to be used for mounting, the switch box may be attached directly to the wall board or plaster by using a special strap. These are available at all electrical supply outlets and are commonly used by electricians for installing new switches in existing buildings.

Connect the two wires to the switch terminals. Fold the excess wire behind the switch and gently force the switch into the box. Secure the switch to the box with the two screws supplied and then install the cover plate. The cover plate should hide the opening cut in the plaster wall. If it doesn't, patch the hole with plaster. Now replace the fuse (or circuit breaker) and try the switch. It works!

REPLACING A WALL SWITCH

THIS IS A COMMON maintenance job because there is no way of actually repairing an outlet whose internal contacts are either loose or burned. All you need in the way of tools are a screwdriver and perhaps a pair of long-nose pliers.

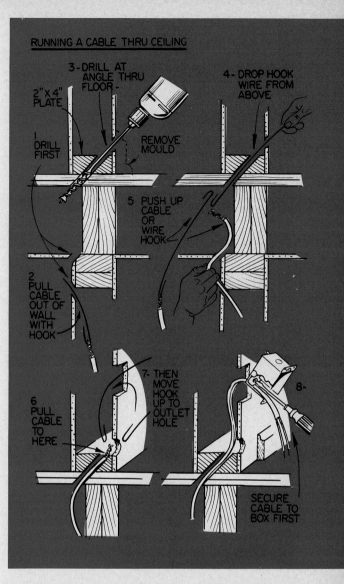

RUNNING A CABLE THRU CEILING

Deactivate power to outlet. Remove screws and pull out old unit. Loosen wire-holding screws and make note of placement. Install new outlet by replacing wires and fastening screws tightly.

Floor and Clock Outlets

To prevent water from entering a floor outlet some have a screw type cover shown below.

IN MANY INSTANCES a floor outlet is absolutely necessary because a lamp or other appliance is located too far from the wall. To extend the cord may not be practical because it would be in the traffic line. This is especially true with open-planned homes where the living and dining areas are one large room.

Many different types of recessed plugs are available to solve such problems. Running the line from the room below is no different than running a regular wall outlet. In fact, in many cases it is easier!

For instance, if you relocate your refrigerator or other appliance and you do not have a nearby wall outlet, it is by far simpler to drill a hole in the floor and install an outlet rather than snake a line through your wall.

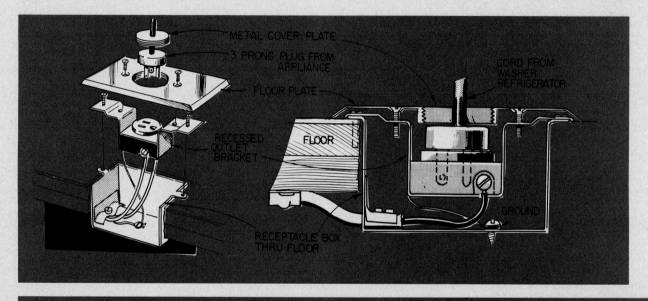

Automatic Closet Light

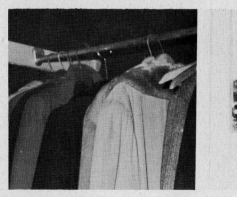

This closet light was recessed into the door jamb when the home was built. Its a permanent job.

MANY CLOSETS have an overhead light, usually operated by a pull-cord. However, pawing around in the darkness to find the elusive string can be very annoying.

There's an easy solution to this problem. In hardware and house furnishings stores you will find several varieties of automatic lights which go on and off with the opening and the closing of the door. Mount the device so that the inside surface of the door, when the latter is shut, presses against a small spring-loaded switch on the lamp socket. Remove the present lamp from the ceiling fixture, replace it with a screw-in plug and insert the plug from the automatic light into it.

A small electric clock draws so little current you need not fear it will overload the circuit.

AN OUTLET for an electric clock must be recessed into the wall so the clock will neatly cover it and still not to prevent the clock from resting flush against the wall. As in the case of floor outlets, a variety of recessed plugs are available for just this purpose. Of course, it is best to plan the location of your wall clocks before building but if you have an existing wall on which you want a timepiece mounted, try to track down nearest outlet, hoping it is in between two of the studs.

Since many kitchen clocks are located above a doorway, unless you remove part of the wall you cannot snake a line laterally without hitting a stud. A better approach is to attempt to run a line from the ceiling above; it will be a snap if you had an attic or crawl space. But if this is impractical then you should investigate some of the new battery powered clocks. They keep accurate time but require a battery change every few months. That is, unless you buy one of the quartz clocks!

CLOCK HOOK
FACE PLATE WITH RECESS FOR OUTLET
OUTLET PUSHED INTO RECESS
RECEPTACLE OVER SINK OR RANGE

GROUND SCREW
CLOCK PLUG
WALL
STEEL CLIP LOCKS IN PLACE
CLOCK

OUTSIDE POWER

It may be possible to use a 120-volt light in a lightless closet if there is an AC outlet on some nearby wall that you can reach by drilling holes in it for a run of lamp cord. Inside walls are plaster over lath or composition panels, and are easy to pierce with a long drill bit. Beware of the possible presence of plastic-sheathed cable in the wall. In many cases you can get a pretty good idea of how the lines run in a wall by opening the outlet, pulling the duplex receptable out carefully, and noting whether the cable runs up and down or sideways. Armored cable is not likely to be damaged by a small drill, as it is quite tough. The instant you feel any resistance to the drill, withdraw it, and start a new hole a few inches away.

LIGHT YOUR WAY INTO YOUR CLOSET
ADJUSTABLE BUTTON SWITCH PUSHED OFF BY DOOR
WIRE RUNS DOWN TO OUTLET

Hanging a Swag Lamp

Hanging from a short chain, this swag lamp is most effective in lighting up a corner decorated with pictures. The height of the lamp can be raised or lowered by adjusting the metal chain as required.

THE USE OF THE TERM "swag" to describe Mediterranean-style electric lamps is relatively new, although the practice of hanging lamps from chains goes back centuries. Swags are very popular because they are decorative, practical and easy to install.

The swag hooks that you can buy where lamps are sold have a head threaded to take a machine screw, usually 10x24. In places along a ceiling where beams or lath can be found (by probing with a slender drill), the actual fastener is a double screw, with machine threads at one end to fit the hook and wood threads at the other to bite into the beam. If the probe goes through the ceiling without hitting wood, you merely have to enlarge the hole to pass a toggle bolt. This is a headless length of threaded rod, one end of which goes into the hook while the other engages a folding butterfly nut. Push the latter end up through the hole; the two wings of the nut press against the rod, and as they clear the upper surface of the ceiling they spring out. To tighten the hook turn clockwise in the usual manner, at the same time pulling down slightly to keep the nut pressed against the ceiling.

If you decide to move a lamp, simply unscrew the swag hooks. The butterfly nut will, of course, be lost.

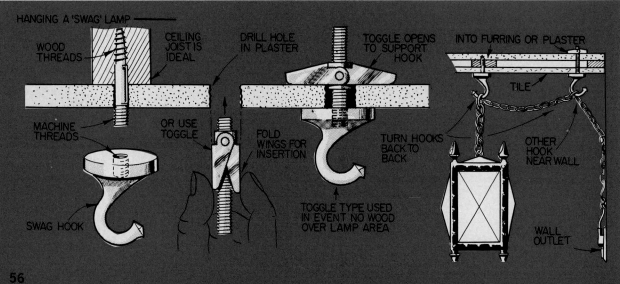

Repairing a Defective Lamp

ONE DAY YOU REPLACE the bulb in a table or floor lamp. You unscrew it and put in a new one, but it doesn't light when you turn on the switch. Is it defective? No, it is okay according to a quick check in another lamp.

Your probable impulse now is to take the lamp apart and look for a broken wire. Wait! Do something much simpler. Unplug the cord, look into the socket and check the condition of the center contact, which is usually a small U-shaped piece of spring brass. It might merely be squashed down too far, or it might be corroded, or it might be broken off. If it is intact, scratch it clean with a small screwdriver, pull it upward a bit with a pair of long-nose pliers, and try the new bulb again.

With half of the contact spring broken off, some sockets still permit the bulb to touch the head of the retaining screw or rivet; others might be a little too short in the neck. A new socket is then the only cure.

To open any standard socket, look for the word "press" near the switch arm. Do as it says, and at the same time wiggle the cap slightly to release its grip. Do *not* twist it. Sometimes it is easier to pry off the cap by means of a thin screwdriver blade poked into the "press" area.

If you have a multimeter, or VOM as they are sometimes called, use it to test the cord for continuity as well as the bulb filament. But an easier way to test the bulb is to try it in another lamp.

The trouble could be in the socket. Remove the plug from the wall outlet and examine the center contact closely. It may be pressed down too far; raise it with the hooked end of a nut picker.

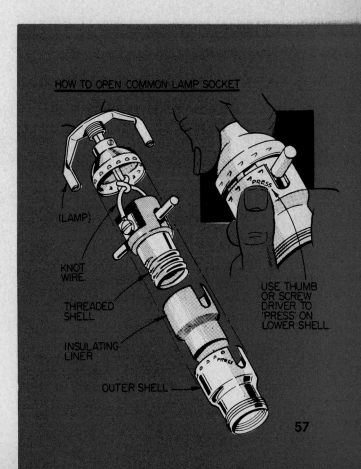

HOW TO OPEN COMMON LAMP SOCKET

(LAMP)

KNOT WIRE

THREADED SHELL

INSULATING LINER

OUTER SHELL

USE THUMB OR SCREWDRIVER TO 'PRESS' ON LOWER SHELL

57

New Lamps from Old Bottles

You can make a lamp worthy of any interior decorator's praise, out of empty beer, liquor, and wine bottles.

WHEN YOU'RE CLEANING up after a party, do you ever get the feeling that it is a downright shame to throw away all those beautiful liquor bottles? It surely is, because with very little effort you can convert some of them into useful and attractive table lamps.

There are two ways of approaching this project. The first is to retain the empties with their labels intact; the lamps then are appropriate for a finished playroom or a man's den. To protect the labels, give them a coating of clear varnish or lacquer. The second is to select bottles that don't look like bottles after their labels have been soaked off in warm water, so that the lamps made from them can be used anywhere in the house. The containers of many imported wines and liquors have very graceful outlines, are made of dark or colored glass, and lend themselves readily to conversion.

Bottles of clear glass can be dressed up by filling them with dilute solutions of tea, coffee, ink, cola drinks, etc. Clean sand is also good because it has an interesting grain pattern and makes the lamp virtually tip-proof.

Adapter kits for electrifying bottles cost about three dollars and are widely available wherever electrical supplies are sold. They consist of a brass lamp socket, a length of wire with a line plug attached, a piece of 3/8-inch threaded brass "nipple" about two inches long, three rubber stoppers an inch long, and a flat washer and a round or hex nut to fit the nipple. The assembly procedure is simple and requires only a screwdriver and a pair of pliers.

Pull the free end of the line cord through the insulated bushing in the cap of the socket and fasten the bared ends of the wire under the connector screws of the inner shell. ("Polarity" is immaterial; either wire can go to the "white" screw, and the other to the brass screw.) Pull gently on the cord to seat the inner shell in the cap, and snap on the outer shell. Screw the nipple into the neck of the socket and place the flat washer over it. Select a stopper that is slightly smaller than the inside diameter of the bottle,

A lamp made out of a booze bottle. After all, after you have enjoyed its contents, there is no reason why it can not be put to further use.

This is a typical adapter kit designed to make a lamp out of a bottle. If you are a teetotaler you can use maple syrup bottle.

The end of the socket assembly is placed over the neck of the bottle and pushed down firmly to seat it in place, as shown.

slide it over the nipple and run the nut over the latter, finger tight. The trick now is to tighten the nut gradually until the stopper jams snugly in the neck of the bottle. The test is to grasp the socket and to see if the bottle holds tight as you raise it off the table.

If one stopper is a trifle too large for a particular bottle and another is too small (that is, it doesn't expand sufficiently when the nut is tightened), use the small one and add a turn or two of tape, the kind used for insulating joints in wires.

The simplest way of supporting the shade for the lamp is by means of a spring that clamps to the electric bulb.

For a more rigid mounting of the shade, use a "harp." This is a closed wire loop, the bottom of which has a 3/8-inch hole through which the nipple in the socket is passed. The top of the loop bears a threaded stud against which the ring of the shade is secured by a decorative nut called a finial.

Small vases also lend themselves to conversion as lamps, but they are more of a problem than bottles because their mouth diameters are rather wide. If a lathe is available in your neighborhood and its services can be "borrowed" on a friendly basis, make a stopper of hardwood, for a snug fit, and secure it with a few drops of epoxy cement.

If a drill press is available, you might consider the possibility of drilling a hole in the side of the bottle or vase, near the bottom. This will permit the line cord to be drawn through the neck of the socket (rather than through the hole in its side), through the mounting nipple, down through the neck of the bottle, and out through the new bottom hole. This arrangement puts the cord at table level and makes the lamp look a little more professional.

Glass drilling isn't as difficult as it sounds. The idea is to build a small retaining wall of putty around the spot where the hole is to be made. In this is spooned a somewhat creamy mixture of Carborundum powder and water. The actual drilling is then done with a short length of tubing, which grinds the abrasive powder through the relatively soft glass. Practice on discarded bottles, to determine the best drill speed and mix consistency.

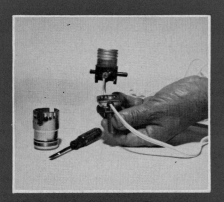

The line cord is passed through a hole in the side of the socket and is connected to the two screws on the inner shell.

The socket is next assembled with the rubber stopper at the bottom. Tightening the nut with pliers causes stopper to expand.

After the wires have been connected to the socket, the next step is to insert the socket end into the neck of the host bottle.

This elegant lamp base, made of black glass, originally contained wine. Its slender neck makes it especially suitable for a lamp.

This converted vase was fitted with a "harp" to hold an extra large shade. Normally the bulb alone supports the shade.

Three "dead soldiers" ready to come to life and do extra duty as lamps for living room, den, or rumpus room. Duty calls!

These timers and electric eyes work constantly. 1. Built-in timer behind removable panel near front door controls entrance lights. 2. With panel off, timer can be adjusted as days get longer and shorter. 3. Typical wall mounted unit resets itself every 24 hours. 4. For indoor use, plug a lamp or radio into this timer. 5. Permanently mounted exterior eyes of different wattage.

Automatic Switches

Timers and electric eyes that operate switches will turn your lights (and motors) on and off at any preset time. A wide variety of built-in and plug-in types are available. They work for you while you sleep.

HAVE YOU EVER GONE OUT in the afternoon with the expectation of returning before dark and then returned much later to find your house dark and unprotected? A problem of this kind will not arise if you invest just a few dollars in a simple and foolproof light-sensitive switch containing a photo-electric cell. Its operation is easily understood. The electrical resistance of the cell varies with the brightness of the light falling on it. The ohmage is low when the light is bright and high when the light is poor. These variations trigger an electronic switch in the circuit to turn off or on any small appliance plugged into the device.

The idea is to place the electric eye near a window so that it "sees" outside light without being blinded by a street lamp or other night-time illumination. Avoid direct exposure to the sun. You can readily experiment with locations, and you can simulate darkness by putting your hand over the eye. With some cells the response to light changes is not instantaneous, but might take several seconds. This is not important, as

the shift from daylight through dusk to darkness is gradual anyway. The "memory" effect in these cells is similar to camera exposure meters. Some of these only measure the light, while others measure it and then automatically set either the lens or the shutter for proper film exposure.

The small bullet-shaped control shown in an accompanying picture represents only one of the many forms now on the market. A very popular photo-electric cell fits the socket of outdoor lamps, without requiring the use of tools for installation. It can also be adapted to porch, garage and garden lights, all of which are excellent security measures around any house.

TIMER SWITCHES

Another automatic control is the clock-operated timer. This turns appliances on and off at pre-set intervals, and keeps repeating itself. It is probably better for inside purposes than for light control; if it turns on room lamps

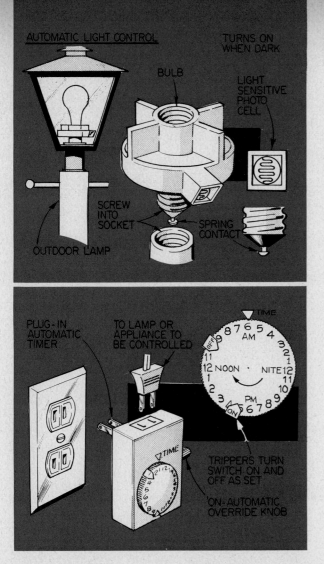

Top drawing shows how a photo-electric cell is used to control an outdoor post lantern. Lower drawing: timer unit plugs into wall outlet for control of indoor lights for predetermined interval.

Another type of clock-timer unit is mounted near the lamp it is to control. It will repeat during any 24-hour interval a regulated "on" and "off" cycle. Use for homes left unoccupied during vacation.

too soon before dark it is less likely to discourage casual sneak thieves than the photo-cell devices do.

A very good combination for control purposes consists of a photo eye *and* a clock timer, with the timer connected to a radio to give the impression of occupancy, and to a fan to circulate air and prevent mildew if the house is left unattended for any length of time.

A clock timer can be rigged to solve the problems of sound sleepers who must get up early but who simply do not respond to ordinary alarm clocks. By means of a cube tap plugged into the outlet of a timer, it is the work of only minutes to hook in a radio set with the volume control turned all the way up, a floor or table lamp with a 150-watt bulb aimed directly over the head of the bed, and a percolator already loaded with water and coffee. If this combination doesn't rouse the sleeper, his neighbors will!

BUY THE RIGHT KIND

In planning the use of timers for household purposes, read the labels carefully before you buy, to be certain that they have adequate power handling capacity. The photo-eye types are generally limited to about 300 watts, which is more than enough for protective lighting. The timer models are better suited for heavier loads. A typical one is marked, "1,875 watts-15 amps-1/4 H.P. motor."

Indoor electric-eye control is inconspicuous and can be mounted permanently if a good spot for it is found by experiment near a window. One line goes to a wall outlet, other line to the lamp.

How to Take Care of Small Appliances

The chances of having your small appliances break down are minimal if you follow these simple maintenance suggestions.

STEAM IRON

AFTER A STEAM IRON has been used for a considerable time it might show symptoms of what is literally hardening of the arteries; that is, the passages become blocked and little or no steam passes. This condition is invariably due to the presence of excessive mineral matter in the water supply. As the water in the iron boils away in the form of steam, the minerals stay behind and are baked to the metal surfaces as hard, rock-like encrustations. There is no way of removing these with a chemical solution. You just have to open the iron and scrape them off by hand.

The actual scraping is easy. The trick is to get the iron apart first. You know that it consists of a number of components, but where are the nuts and bolts that hold them together? Look directly under the handle. Is there a decorative name plate or instruction plate here? Pry it off with a knife, and you're pretty sure to find a large nut or screw head. Loosening this can be a problem because of heat-created corrosion. However, a couple of drops of *Liquid Wrench* (an effective penetrating oil) applied to the

CAN OPENER

MANY WEDDING GIFTS end up in a closet, but the lowly can opener goes to work quickly in the newlyweds' kitchen. If hubby expects to eat regularly, it behooves him to keep the appliance in good order.

The heart of a can opener is a small, high-speed motor. By means of a series of reduction gears, this drives a toothed wheel that presses the lip of a can against a cutting wheel having a sharp V-shaped rim. As the running time per can is usually only about five seconds, the motor can be expected to have a very long life. In fact, in some models there is no provision for replacing the carbon brushes. The manufac-turers probably figure that the machine will outlive the marriage!

For smooth cutting, the two little wheels should be cleaned regularly. A stiff toothbrush is fine for the purpose. If food that oozes out of the cans is allowed to harden, you might have to scrape it off with the point of a small knife. Do not oil the wheels; they cut better dry.

In some openers one end of the motor shaft extends out of the case and is fitted with a small grinding wheel for sharpening knives. This is of limited usefulness because it is shrouded for safety and the knife cannot be drawn across it evenly for its full length. Before trusting an expensive knife to this treatment, experiment with a more expendable one.

COFFEE POT

THE BOTTOM COVER of most coffee makers is secured to the heating section of the pot by a single large bolt in the center or sometimes two smaller screws. If these are removed, the prongs that take the detachable line cord become accessible. These connectors carry a heavy current, and will not overheat if they are kept tight and bright.

Do not attempt to clean or adjust any small open contact springs connected between the prongs and the sealed heating element. These springs are part of the thermostat that controls the percolating cycle of the water in the pot.

threads usually enables a wrench or a screwdriver to do the job.

With this first fastener out, the handle and cover assembly should lift away, with the line cord still connected to the heating coils in the sole plate. The next step is to remove the water reservoir, which is shaped to conform to the plate. Again, look for a large screw, which usually is in the filler neck through which the water is poured. Note carefully the positions of the various parts that come loose, so that you can reassemble them later.

With reservoir off, you can now examine the sole plate and clean it as needed. Do not disturb the thermostat, which is easy to identify because it is situated near the line cord terminals.

The obvious way to avoid trouble with hard water is to treat it with a water softener. A powder packaged specifically for steam-iron purposes is available in supermarkets and hardware stores.

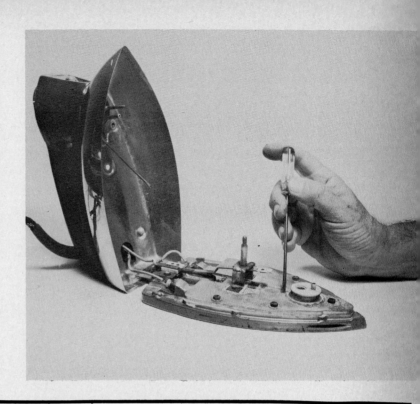

If you are curious about the internal construction of this appliance, don't hesitate to remove the mounting screws on the back or the bottom and to pry off the cover. *With the plug out of the outlet, in case you've forgotten!* You'll observe that the gear train is well covered with a sticky lubricant. Check the insulation on the line cord at the point where the latter enters the case. If it shows any sign of wear, reinforce it with a bit of tape. Also, press a clean rag against the commutator and rotate the shaft by hand, to clean off any excess carbon dust.

When parts wear out or break you may be tempted to scrap the appliance. But before you do, check with your Yellow Pages for a Small Appliance Parts dealer.

TOASTER

If the toaster is checked regularly, perhaps once a month, a cleaning with a soft brush will keep it in proper operating condition. If the brush cannot be pushed in far enough to reach some crumbs on the slice holders, try an air blast from a reversed vacuum cleaner. Before applying the hose to the toaster, let it run free for a minute or so to clear out its own dust.

A toaster that has been neglected for a long time might have to be taken apart for a thorough cleaning. Most models are held together with self-tapping screws and can be disassembled readily. The accompanying illustrations show what can be done

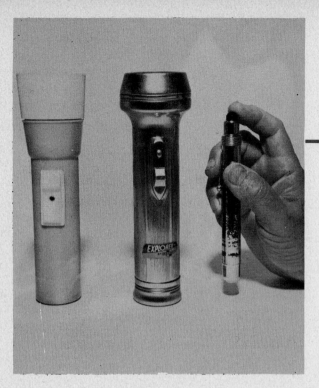

Keep Your Flashlight in Condition

There is nothing so frustrating as to pick up a flashlight and find out it won't even glow. Why did the battery fail?

AROUND THE HOUSE, a flashlight is a sort of emergency tool, for use during power failures, to light the way to the baby's room or the bathroom without awakening the kids or your spouse, to find coins and other items that roll under furniture, to change a fuse and similar jobs. Most of the time it is half-forgotten in a kitchen drawer or in the glove compartment of the family car, but when you need it—you really need it—and it should be ready.

The bulb rarely burns out, because a flashlight is usually "on" for short periods. The batteries are what require attention. Their "shelf life" is quite long, but they do tend to dry out with time. Turn the light on and you can tell quickly if the batteries need replacement.

Also examine them closely for signs of leakage. This takes the form of a sticky goo, usually white or gray, that attacks nearby parts such as the switch, the contact springs, the lamp housing, and the shell of the flashlight itself if it is of metal. Worse yet, leakage means that the batteries are dead and swelling. Once they get jammed inside it is virtually impossible to dislodge them. You can save the bulb, but the case is generally a total loss.

When buying new batteries, look for the all-metal sealed type and avoid cheap bargains made in the Orient. The name-brand American manufacturers have improved the construction of their batteries to the point where some of them now carry one of the best guarantees in the electrical business. Here's a typical one: "If your flashlight is damaged by corrosion, leakage or swelling of this battery, send it to us with the batteries and we will give you free a new comparable flashlight with batteries." Can't beat that, can you?

The most widely sold flashlight is the two-cell type. The batteries are known as D cells and are 1 1/4 inches in diameter and 2 1/4 inches high. There are also three- and five-cell models for special purposes.

Another type of two-cell flashlight, called the "pen-light" because it resembles an overgrown fountain pen, is popular for pocket or purse use. This uses the small AA cells, which are a half-inch in diameter and two inches long.

Flashlight batteries are classified technically as "dry," but this is only a relative term. They contain chemicals in paste form which can dry out long in advance of the normal expiration date if they are subjected to excessive heat. In practical terms, this means that you shouldn't hang a flashlight near the furnace, the kitchen range or a radiator. By the same token, protect it against freezing.

If you need to use one outdoors in very cold weather, keep it in an inside pocket as much as possible when it isn't actually on.

To get at the innards of a plastic style flashlight, you must unscrew the top end—the part that contains the bulb and reflector. Remove these and you can now remove the two batteries for replacement.

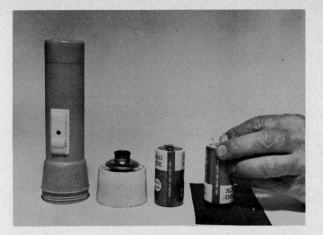

Sometimes, just taking a flashlight apart and cleaning the battery ends and the tip of the bulb (by rubbing over fine sandpaper) will improve its performance. Remove dead batteries to avoid rust.

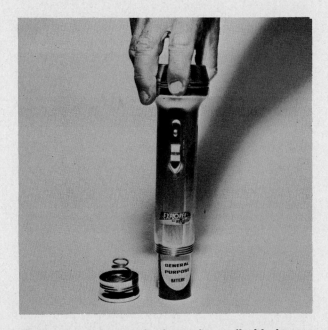

Both ends of the standard metal case flashlight can be removed. Unscrew the bottom cap for access to the batteries; unscrew the top end for access to the bulb and reflector. Clean and reinstall.

The bulb is generally mounted inside a small housing to protect it from the pressure of the batteries. Turn the end of the housing slightly counter-clockwise to release bulb for examination and cleaning.

Watch the polarity of the batteries! Always insert batteries with the "plus" or center post facing the bulb. Then insert the second battery so its center post touches the "minus" end of first battery.

Slender pen-light is open at both ends. Left to right: 1. Plastic retainer of bulb. 2. Special bulb with concentrating bead tip. 3. Case with pocket clip. 4. Two "AA" cells. 5. End cap with switch.

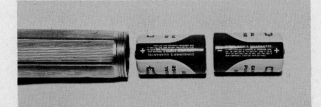

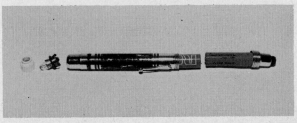

Below: a small two-tone door chime. It strike one note when button is pushed and another note when it is released. Right: a four-tube chime that strikes eight notes and can be set to strike only four notes if desired.

Door Chimes

Instead of a raucus doorbell, melodious chimes can now announce the arrival of a bill collector.

IN MOST NEW HOMES melodious chimes are taking the place of the raucous bell-and-buzzer combination that dates back to the time of dry cells. It is easy to make a change-over in older houses because the existing wiring and door buttons can be used. All that is needed are the chimes and a new transformer.

The standard operating voltage of chimes is 16 volts. Note in the diagram that the chimes and the buttons are wired to the 16-volt secondary of the line transformer, and that the primary of the transformer is connected permanently to the AC source. This is perfectly safe because it draws only a very small current.

The chimes themselves consist of open brass tubes that are struck by magnetically operated little hammers when the pushbutton is pressed. The chimes peal once when the button is pressed and a second time when it is released.

TROUBLE SHOOTING

Because it is in use for short and infrequent periods, a door signaling system lasts practically forever. When it does stop working, the trouble in 99 cases out of 100, is a corroded door but-ton. The internal parts of some buttons are made of iron and they inevitably rust. Unscrew a suspected button from the wall and try short-circuiting the terminals with a clean screwdriver blade; if the chimes come to life, buy a new button. Incidentally, you might as well buy one of the illuminated type. A tiny bulb under the button is connected to the button's terminals, thus connecting it to the transformer. Enough current flows through this complete circuit to light the bulb, but not enough to ring the chimes. When the button is pressed, the resistance of the lamp is shorted out by the button's contacts, and the chimes peal.

CLEANING

If the chimes' box is mounted on a kitchen wall it is bound to accumulate grease from cooking vapors. It therefore should be inspected about every six months and cleaned if necessary. Don't be surprised if you find insect nests in the tubes.

What to do with a six-volt transformer from a bell system after you replace it by a 16-volt unit? Save it for use with electric trains and small toys.

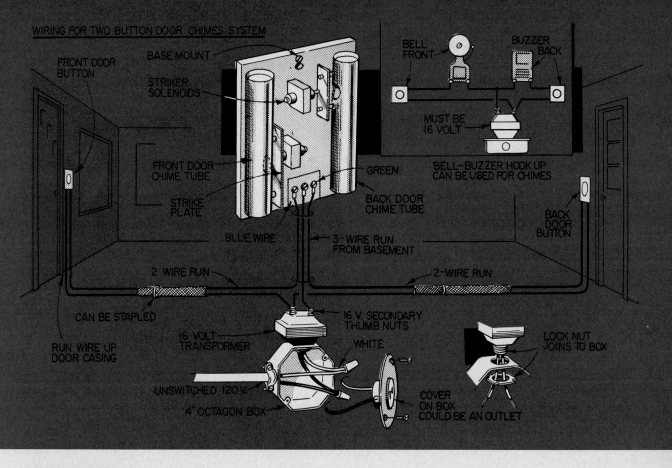

WIRING FOR TWO BUTTON DOOR CHIMES SYSTEM

FRONT DOOR BUTTON

BASE MOUNT

STRIKER SOLENOIDS

FRONT DOOR CHIME TUBE

STRIKE PLATE

BLUE WIRE

GREEN

BACK DOOR CHIME TUBE

3-WIRE RUN FROM BASEMENT

2-WIRE RUN

2-WIRE RUN

CAN BE STAPLED

RUN WIRE UP DOOR CASING

16 VOLT TRANSFORMER

16 V. SECONDARY THUMB NUTS

WHITE

UNSWITCHED 120 V.

4" OCTAGON BOX

COVER ON BOX COULD BE AN OUTLET

BELL FRONT

BUZZER BACK

MUST BE 16 VOLT

BELL-BUZZER HOOK UP CAN BE USED FOR CHIMES

BACK DOOR BUTTON

LOCK NUT JOINS TO BOX

If chimes are not working, the first place to look for trouble is at pushbutton. Remove it from door jamb and short circuit the terminals. If the chimes work, then the pushbutton is at fault.

Below: all chimes operate on a 16-volt transformer. Check here for loose wires. Caution: do not use a 6-volt transformer which may have been used to power an old-fashioned door bell.

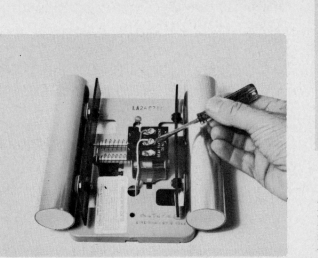

Left: Another possible cause of trouble may be loose wire on the chime unit itself. Also, make sure that the plungers which strike the chime tubes are operating freely. Use graphite, not oil.

An intercom system for your entire house will save steps and permit you to interview callers at your front door without leaving the kitchen. This Nutone unit also has a built-in AM-FM radio.

Located adjacent the front door, this speaker and microphone is weatherproof. After ringing your doorbell, when you answer the caller can speak by tripping the outside spring-loaded switch.

Intercoms-the Great Step Savers

You can't beat an intercom system for finding out who is at the front door—without taking a step!

AN INTERCOM SYSTEM in the home is a step saver, a voice saver, a baby sitter and a security measure. In its simplest form it comprises a "master" unit containing a voice amplifier, a small loud speaker that also functions as a microphone, and a couple of controls; and a "remote," which is merely a loudspeaker in a box, with no controls of any kind. The amplifier can be AC or battery operated.

You should understand that home-type intercoms differ from conventional telephones as only one person can speak at a time, controlled by the master. Technically, this is called "simplex" operation, as distinguished from "duplex" telephone operation wherein both parties can yak away at will. Furthermore, only the master can initiate a call, by turning the unit on and pushing a switch marked, Press To Talk. When he wants an answer, he merely releases the switch and allows the remote to speak. If he leaves the power switch on and doesn't touch the talk switch, he can eavesdrop on everything said in the vicinity of the remote. This feature makes even a low-priced intercom invaluable as a baby sitter.

The one-way control arrangement has one disadvantage. Consider an intercom between a basement workshop and the kitchen of a house. You might want to ask your wife if lunch is in the making, or she might anticipate the question by wanting to tell you that it is. If the remote is in the kitchen, you can't alert her to turn it on, or if it's in the basement she can't alert you to do the same.

However, the one-way deal is ideal for an important application: communication between the front door of a house and the kitchen, the room most likely to be occupied during the day. If the doorbell rings, the person in the kitchen has only to flip the intercom on, press the talk switch, and say, "Yes, who is it?"

There is virtually no limit to the number of remotes than can be tied to a single master. All the latter needs is the appropriate number of switch positions.

For more flexibility and convenience, there are numerous systems in which remotes can alert the master even with the latter off. However, with most intercoms it is not practical to have direct talking *between* remotes. A simple relay system often serves the same purpose. For example, a daughter in an upstairs bedroom wants to know if her mother in the basement laundry has a certain article of clothing in the washer. If some other member of the family is in or near the kitchen, she buzzes the latter and explains the problem. Master buzzes the laundry, gets the answer, and then calls

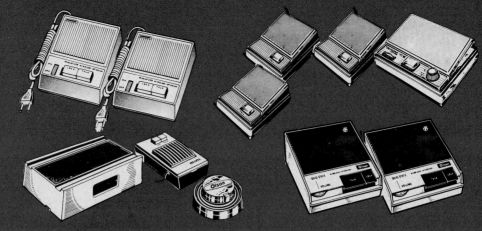

This selection of wireless intercoms by Olson Electronics is applicable in home and office alike. Plugged into a regular AC outlet in your home, apartment or office, you communicate immediately!

back to the bedroom. This is certainly much less work than running down and up stairs.

Self-contained intercoms generally run on a single nine-volt battery of the type commonly used in small solid-state radio receivers. Most AC models take so little current (about as much as for an electric clock) that they can be left on more or less permanently.

The monitoring capability of many intercoms, even small and inexpensive ones, is nothing short of extraordinary. The remote unit of a door-to-kitchen installation can often pick up children's voices 50 yards away and make them perfectly intelligible in the loud speaker of the master.

THE "WIRELESS" INTERCOM

The only problem in intercom installation is the station-to-station wiring. While the wire is thin and easily concealed, it must still be pulled through walls or windows and draped around door frames. This work is completely unnecessary with a very interesting type of intercom called "wireless." Masters and remotes are identical little radio "transceivers"(that is, combination *trans*mitter and *receivers*) that are simply plugged into any of the AC outlets of a house and provide intercom facilities the instant they are turned on. All the units of a particular system are tuned to a low frequency, far below the standard AM broadcast band. The voice signals travel over the house wiring rather than through the air, without interference to or from the AC.

The only limitation on wireless intercoms is that they must be used in buildings fed by the same distribution transformer. The latter tends to prevent the signals from passing through to another transformer that feeds other buildings.

Plug in and talk! The applications of the system are almost endless. Some models offer not merely one but two or three independent channels. Many have internal "squelch" adjustments that silence the loudspeaker when no signals are incoming. This is especially desirable when a system is left on continuously for monitoring purposes, such as baby sitting. Without squelch there is often an annoying background of line noise.

Because of the ease of setting up, wireless intercoms are great for temporary applications: in a sick room, to keep a patient in close touch with the family; in a back-yard garage, to permit monitoring of the front door; in a basement darkroom, to keep the occupant from getting lonesome in the gloom; and so forth.

It is also entirely practical for cooperative neighbors to organize a remote baby-sitting system, with one wireless intercom next to the crib and the other in a neighbor's house. Thus, the residents of the latter can carry on as usual and still hear every breath the child takes. This is often better than trusting the baby to a teenage sitter who is more concerned with the family's refrigerator than with the child.

It is interesting to experiment with wireless intercoms and to determine just how far and how well they carry from room to room and from house to house. This information can be valuable when members of a community decide to arrange a security radio net to protect houses that are temporarily unoccupied. One unit in the living room, monitored by a neighbor anywhere within the predetermined range, can help to discourage burglary or vandalism and to bring police to the scene in a hurry if necessary.

Since master and remote of a wireless intercom contain the same electronic components, the price of a pair is bound to be higher than that of a wired system, but the advantages are obvious. Base price of a two-station wired outfit is about $15; of a wireless model, about $35.

The Refrigerator and Freezer

These indispensable appliances are virtually trouble-free, but there are still a few important maintenance and purchasing points you should know.

BECAUSE THE MACHINERY of refrigerators is complicated and most of it is sealed up and not readily accessible, there is very little a home owner can do to this important kitchen accessory except to keep it clean, inside and out. It requires no initial preparation for installation; only a nearby 120-volt outlet. Wheel it in, plug it in, set the internal thermostat, and in a short time it is cold.

SETTING IT UP

The things you *can* do are simple. Manufacturers strongly advise leveling the machine just after its arrival and again a month or two later, after it has had a chance to settle onto the surface of the floor. In some models there are adjustable leveling feet in all four corners of the base; some larger refrigerator-freezers have the back legs on rollers to make them easier to move and only the front corners are adjustable.

The only maintenance job is cleaning either the back or the bottom, where the heat exchanger coils are located. The dust accumulated here is gulped up in seconds by a vacuum cleaner.

Freezers are no different than refrigerators other than the fact that they are designed to provide a constant temperature of 0 degrees (the average temperature of the refrigerator food storage area is 40 degrees). Just about every household in the country has one (or perhaps two) refrigerators, and the manufacturers are building so many improvements into the newer models we consumers are often tempted to discard our six-year-old box for a new one that has built-in ice cube maker, cold water dispenser, air-tight compartment for vegetables and the likes.

One of the big selling points of the newer refrigerators and freezers is the "frostless" feature. Just about all of the models sold today are of this type, and they do indeed save time and mess of regular defrosting.

Ever wonder how a defroster works? The op-

The machinery; inside a refrigerator will run more smoothly and the doors will close more easily if the box is level. Note open grille work along bottom; this is for dissipation of heat.

With the bottom grille unsnapped, it only takes a minute to clean out the heat exchanger of the refrigerator. This area attracts insects, dust and lint so the job should be done fairly often.

The most popular refrigerator has a top freezer compartment with up to 6-cubic foot capacity. All the newer appliances have magnetic gaskets that provide a tight seal when the door is closed.

This side-by-side combination refrigerator-freezer by Frigidare does the same job as freezer boxes but has a slightly larger freezer capacity. One compressor runs both sections of appliance.

eration is really simple and involves a small electric timer that operates a simple single-pole, double-throw switch. During the day when the refrigerator is opened and closed many times, the switch is in the lower position; this completes the circuit to the motor operated compressor-condenser-fan combination and the interior stays at the temperature determined by its thermostat. However, during the during the early hours of the morning, when the family is usually asleep, the timer flips the switch to the upper position which cuts the cooling unit off the hot line and transfers power to the defroster heaters. These give the freezer compartment a flash of heat, just enough to melt any ice formed from vapor but not enough to defrost frozen food or harmfully increase the temperature of food in the refrigerator section.

You can conclude from this brief explanation that all the "frostless" or "self defrost" feature require is electricity—so you should expect increased electric bills from this type of equipment. Obviously, the cost of running a self-defrost box is greater than that of a no-defrost unit having the same cubic foot of space. However, since the efficiency of units by different manufacturers vary, so does their monthly cost of operation. So ask your dealer or utility company just what any individual make of refrigerator or freezer, should cost to operate. That is, if you want to save money!

If you require freezer capacity well in excess of 6-cubic feet, upright single door and chest types, are available. The upright model is preferred because it takes up less floor space.

A washing machine and dryer combination is the greatest labor-saver in the home. The washer requires a 15-amp, 120-volt circuit but the dryer, if electric needs a 240-volt, 20 to 30-amp circuit.

The Clothes Washer

The Dryer

The most important requirement with these appliances is to make certain you have the correct power and, of course, the right plumbing.

OF ALL THE ELECTRICAL appliances now on the market, the two most appreciated · by housewives are the clothes washer and its companion dryer. Both are reliable and give long service *providing they are not overloaded.* Other than its obvious need for water and drain connections, the washer is electrical in operation, while the dryer might use either electricity or gas.

Virtually all washers work satisfactorily off any standard 120-volt, 15-ampere outlet on a power line protected by either a slow-blow fuse or a circuit breaker. So do all gas-heated dryers, as the motor is the only electrical load. Most all-electric dryers for installation in private homes require a separate 240-volt branch circuit protected to 30 or 50 amperes.

Many people start their home laundries with a washer, but add a dryer when they realize that it frees them of the problem of what to do with a tub full of wet wash on a rainy, snowy or freezing day. There is often a tangible saving in buying a matched pair of machines.

PORTABLE WASHERS AND DRYERS

For use in small homes or in apartments, there are under-sized, semi-portable, plug-in type washers and dryers that offer the same labor-saving features of larger models. The

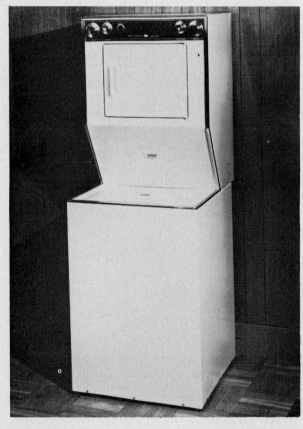

Ideal for the small family, this Frigidare combination unit is only 24" wide and runs on a 15-amp, 120-volt circuit. Washer unit is at the bottom; dryer is at the top to make loading easy.

water hook-up is made by a flexible hose between the washer and the kitchen faucet, while the drain pipe is simply hung over the sink. The dryer is invariably all-electric, as it is not safe or practical to use a detachable gas line. The wattage rating of a typical dryer is about the same as that of a grille or a toaster, so the machine can be plugged into a 120-volt outlet protected to 15 or preferably 20 amperes. Any other appliances on the same circuit should be turned off while the dryer is running.

PERMANENT TYPES

The laundry section or the utility room of most new houses is provided with garden-hose type faucets for hot and cold water and a ver-

tical drain pipe standing between them into which the U-shaped drain hose of the washer is hooked. With these facilities, it shouldn't take more than 15 minutes after unpacking to have a washer doing its first load.

VENTING

A dryer takes a bit more work, because its four-inch diameter vent pipe must eventually terminate at a hole in an outside wall of the house. You don't know how much moisture a tub of towels can hold until you try to run the machine without this external outlet; the room will be a duplicate of a Turkish bath. For the semi-portable models use an optional window-vent kit that includes five or six feet of flexible four-inch hose.

The hot and cold water hose connections to the washer should be readily accessible so the unit can be disconnected for service. In fact, it is good practice to turn the water off after use.

Washers and dryers have separate plugs. The plug at the left is for the 240-volt dryer while the right plug is for the washer. Both appliances should be grounded to a nearby cold water pipe.

Discharge hose of the washer should dump into an adjacent tub or sink about 34" high. If the appliance is in the kitchen the plumbing connection can be made in the wall behind machine.

If you lack space or do not want a permanent installation, this clever arrangement by Whirlpool may solve your problem. The top dryer section remains in place; washer is rolled to the sink.

The Electric Range

Imposing and important, the electric range is surprisingly easy to maintain. Here are tips on how to keep your range in tip-top condition.

ALTHOUGH IT IS BIG and imposing-looking, the range is a rather simple electrical appliance. Except for its timer, which is merely a clock-operated switch, it has no moving parts and is easy to maintain. In fact, maintenance consists largely of keeping the heating elements clean and checking the line plug and the wall outlet for a tight fit.

The possibility of burn-out of heating elements is remote because of their rugged construction, but "possibility" means what it says. To acquaint yourself with their assembly, don't hesitate to lift one loose by means of a screwdriver. You will observe that it has four terminals, which are switched around by the heat controls to give several temperatures. The wires to the terminals are thick, but just flexible enough to permit the whole element to rise above the surface of the range. Inspect it closely, and you'll readily figure out what screws you have to loosen to release the element for replacement.

The connection to the AC line is often neglected because it is usually under the range in a dish compartment. The line "cord" is a short length of heavy armored cable containing three No. 6 wires, fused for 50 amps.

PILOT LIGHT

A small but important item that must not be overlooked is the pilot light on the control panel, as this is the reminder that one, several, or all of the burners are on. To get at it you probably have to remove the entire cover of the panel, which is usually held only by a couple of screws along its edges. If the panel includes a timer, you may also have to remove the little knobs of the setting handles, which are held only by friction and come off by pulling them. It's a good idea to keep an extra light on hand, so that you can make an immediate replacement when necessary.

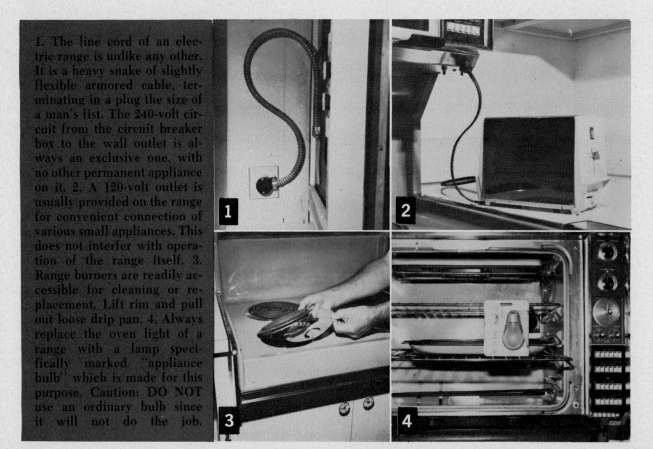

1. The line cord of an electric range is unlike any other. It is a heavy snake of slightly flexible armored cable, terminating in a plug the size of a man's fist. The 240-volt circuit from the circuit breaker box to the wall outlet is always an exclusive one, with no other permanent appliance on it. 2. A 120-volt outlet is usually provided on the range for convenient connection of various small appliances. This does not interfere with operation of the range itself. 3. Range burners are readily accessible for cleaning or replacement. Lift rim and pull out loose drip pan. 4. Always replace the oven light of a range with a lamp specifically marked "appliance bulb" which is made for this purpose. Caution: DO NOT use an ordinary bulb since it will not do the job.

Ideally, exhaust fans are built into a hood directly above the stove and have a 2-speed motor. Fans are rated by CFM, indicating how many Cubic Feet of air they can move per Minute. They come in two versions. The ventless type has a charcoal-filter for odor removal. This Nutone unit also has lights.

Kitchen Ventilators

When vented to the outdoors, exhaust fans can remove odors, smoke. But if you can't extend duct work outside, odors are removed by a charcoal filter.

Roof and exterior wall mounted fans are preferred because the motor noise is kept outdoors. They are available in all sizes to ventilate a complete room. This Nutone is rated at 1000 CFM.

DOES YOUR LIVING ROOM smell of fried fish before, after, and during dinner? Well, lots of people like fish, but not its aroma during preparation. And about the only way you can get rid of fish-cooking odors—as well as other culinary smells—is by means of a kitchen exhaust fan, or some sort of duct system using a fan to dispel the smell somewheres else in the neighborhood.

The simplest type of ventilating system for the kitchen is a window fan installed so that it blows *out*, not in. Not too practical, as the fan will hide a good deal of the landscape facing the window. A better idea is the installation of

a through-the-wall fan. A job not as hard as it seems as these fans come with a sleeve, ready for insertion in the wall, after you have cut the required opening. The opening in the wall will depend upon the fan size.

There are two types of wall fans available. The most common is operated by a pull chain. Releasing the chain opens up the protective cover on the outside of the house and turns on the fan motor. Pulling the chain turns off the current and closes the cover. A more sophisticated version is controlled by a wall switch. Flipping the switch on, opens the cover and turns on the fan.

The Disposal

Waste disposals save work in the kitchen. They are prohibited in some communities, mandatory in others.

A DISPOSAL IS A MOTOR-OPERATED chopper, attached to the bottom of a kitchen sink, that grinds food remnants into small pieces and flushes them down the drain. It has its limitations as to what it can take without choking, but it is popular with housewives who like to minimize the use of a garbage pail.

If you're thinking of adding a disposal to your sink, first check with the local building authorities and determine if it is permissable. In many communities faced with problems of solid waste disposition, disposals are not allowed and appliances dealers in the area probably don't even carry them.

INSTALLATION

The installation of a disposal is primarily a plumbing job, as it calls for the removal and rerouting of existing pipes. This is awkward rather than difficult because of the limited

Undersink disposals require a simple plumbing hookup and a 15-amp electrical connection. The disposal works only when a switch is tripped. Sealed 1/3 HP and ½ HP units are available.

working space under the sink. You also, have to provide an outlet for power. Depending on the size of the motor, the current draw is about 5 to 10 amperes. Since a disposal is operated for only a minute or so at a time, it is practical to tap into a nearby 120-volt outlet for power.

RESET BUTTON

Most disposals are equipped with a circuit breaker to protect the motor from burning out if it stalls on such undigestible items as steak bones and spoons. For some unknown reason manufacturers usually put this important device on the side or back of the disposal, where it often cannot be seen. Investigate with a flashlight and a mirror so that you'll know where to find the reset button the first time the machine quits.

Clearing a disposal of obstructions can be a real fishing expedition. Before you do anything else, turn off the power. You can now probe with your fingers or a pair of long-nose pliers or a loop made of coat-hanger wire.

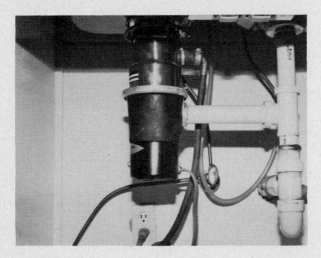

While it is best to install a disposal at the time the rough plumbing is installed, the lines can be easily cut in if your plumbing is in place. If the grinder jams it can be freed very easily.

The Compactor

Refuse compactors help the homeowner and collector alike. The electrical connection is simple, and the unit lasts a lifetime.

LEAVE IT TO THE MANUFACTURERS of electrical appliances to dream up new machines that save time and labor for the American housewife—and her husband. An appliance that is becoming increasingly popular because it does an unusual job and is relatively trouble-free is the compactor. This looks like a dish washer, but is slightly smaller. The internal mechanism consists of piston-like ram driven into a strong metal bucket by a geared-down motor of about 1/3 horsepower. Thus, the machine can be plugged into any 15-amp branch circuit protected by the usual slow-blow fuse or a circuit breaker.

The idea is to put loose trash into a bag in the bucket and to let the ram squeeze it down to *one-quarter* of its original volume. Some models have a built-in deodorizer that sprays each batch of garbage as the front door is closed. The disposable container is either a plastic or heavy paper bag. However, many users find it practical to compact the trash directly into the metal bucket and to empty the latter into a garbage can that can take several such loads.

IS IT NOISY?

The compactor supplements but does not replace the disposal. It is intended primarily to handle bottles, cans, cartons and loose paper, all of which are a problem in any household because they take up so much space. As you might expect, the machine makes quite a racket, but only for one minute or less, as it crunches everything flat.

HOW ABOUT GLASS?

To prevent pieces of broken glass from puncturing the bag, it is advisable to put bottles in the center, surrounded if possible, by cartons or paper. Actually, this isn't as much of a danger as it sounds, because the ram comes down slowly.

The weight of a full bag is about 25 to 35 pounds, for an average family of four for about five or six days. Cost of electricity is negligible because the running cycle is so short.

Like any other food container, a compactor must be kept clean to discourage bugs. The mechanisms of all models are designed for easy removal and washing.

Excellent safety precautions are an essential part of compactors. The machine cannot start if the bag drawer is open or if the key is not in the AC line lock-switch. After each cycle the ram returns to its uppermost position and the motor shuts off.

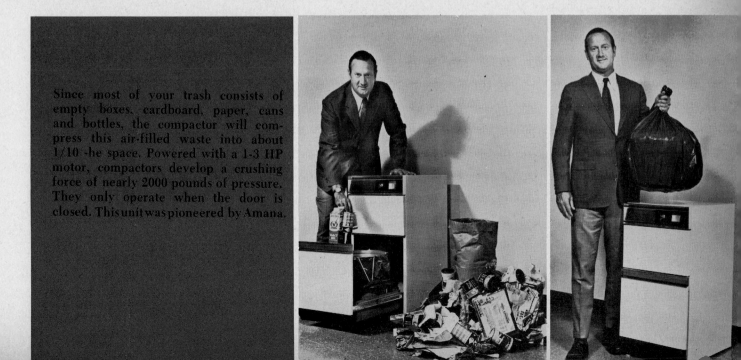

Since most of your trash consists of empty boxes, cardboard, paper, cans and bottles, the compactor will compress this air-filled waste into about 1/10 the space. Powered with a 1-3 HP motor, compactors develop a crushing force of nearly 2000 pounds of pressure. They only operate when the door is closed. This unit was pioneered by Amana.

Electric Water Heaters

Your water heater will eventually develop a leak, which calls for replacement. Until that time, here are a few tips to keep it functioning.

IT IS EASY to take an electric water heater for granted and to pay it no heed, because it contains no moving parts and is absolutely silent in operation. However, there are two simple things you can do to keep it working and to increase its life.

One. All heaters work on 240 volts and take a lot of amperes. Therefore, it is important to have a very good connection between the prongs of the line plug and the contact springs of the wall outlet. Usually, just sliding the plug in and out several times about once a month is enough to prevent corrosion from forming. Every six months or so it is a good idea to polish the prongs and the springs with an emery board, borrowed from your wife's toilet kit. Open the line's circuit breaker before poking around in the wall outlet.

Two. It might not be in open sight, but there is a thermostat somewhere on the heater. Look for a plate held by small screws. Remove these and the plate and you'll expose an inner blanket of fluffy thermal insulation. Pull this apart carefully and the thermostat will reveal itself. The markings on the scale represent the approximate temperature to which the thermostat can be set.

WHICH SETTING TO USE?

Experiment with different settings to determine which one satisfies the requirements of your family. The lower the temperature, the longer the life of the tank and the lower the electric bills. However, if it is too low, a single bath or one load of dishes in a washer might exhaust the tank and make you wait an hour before fresh water heats up.

The water should not be hot enough to scald the skin or to form wisps of steam as it leaves a tap. For ordinary bathing and washing purposes it should be hot enough to require mixing with some cold water. With such a thermostat setting, the tank will retain sufficient hot water for a quick second bath or wash.

SIZES

The bigger the heater, the greater its reserve capacity and the smaller the chance that it will run cold at some inopportune time such as when your in-laws come a-visiting. Remember this when you must consider the possibility of replacing your present model. The standard sizes are of 30-, 42-, 52-, 66- and 82-gallon capacity.

Panel at heater base contains a temperature control device which is preset at the factory. When buying a new heater make certain it has a built-in high-limit cut-off should the thermostat fail.

Your water temperature can be increased or decreased by merely turning the thermostat screw. Tuck in insulation and screw back the panel. Mark the temperature setting on the outside.

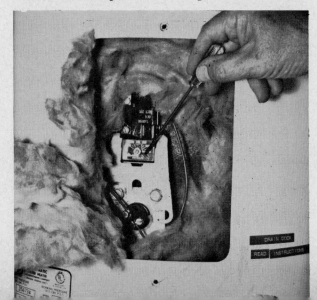

Bathroom Heaters

After a hot bath or shower, you will feel more comfortable with an extra boost of heat. Plug-in and built-in ceiling and wall heaters do the job.

A ceiling heater-light is much safer than a portable heater because it eliminates the possibility of body contact. Three bulb radiant heaters (as shown in inset) also provide instant heat.

A COMMON design fault in many two-story houses is the placement of the bathroom at the very end of the heating line from the furnace in the basement. This room is the last to warm up, and it can get very uncomfortable during the winter. The only virtue in the situation is that occupants don't stay behind the locked door any longer than absolutely necessary.

Many home owners find it expedient to depend on a portable electric heater. This is practical because most bathrooms are small, have small windows (if any), and therefore tend to retain heat once it is furnished in adequate volume. There's no installation problem. A heater is a simple appliance and merely plugs into a wall outlet.

Heaters are rated according to their power requirements in watts. A typical low-priced one-heat model (about $10) takes 1,320 watts and depends on a polished aluminum reflector behind the heating elements to throw its warning rays outward. Larger models have built-in fans to circulate the warm air (a highly desirable feature), thermostats to keep the temperature within desired limits, and multi-heat controls. For mild weather a low setting of 1,000 watts might be enough; for colder weather, settings of 1,320 and 1,640 watts might be more comfortable. The last figure represents the maximum that can be drawn safely from a branch circuit.

A safety feature common to most portable heaters is a tip-over switch. This cuts off the current if the appliance is knocked over accidentally. Actually, there is very little danger of either fire or shock with modern heaters because the heating elements, which glow a bright red, are well protected behind steel wire grilles.

Of course, portable heaters are not limited to the bathroom. They are invaluable also in rooms which must be kept warm for the benefit of bed-ridden children or adults, at times when the central heating system of the house is normally off.

Heaters require virtually no maintenance except cleaning. However, it is important to warn all members of the family not to step on the line cord or to splash water into the case.

CEILING HEATERS

Of course if you want to really doll up your bathroom, you can opt for a ceiling heater that not only has a built-in light, but also a ventilating system. The built-in light is important, as many homeowners can remove the ceiling light in the bathroom and install the combination heater and light. One company, Nutone, makes more than a dozen models—with lights, without lights and with or without a ventilating system.

The units with the ventilating systems are especially important with bathrooms which do not have windows for ventilation. Useful accessories include timer-switches which will turn off the heater after a preset time interval—important as the natural tendency is to turn off the light when leaving the bathroom—and completely forgetting about the heat that may still be on. Timer switches vary from 15-minutes to 60-minute settings (you select from one to 60 minutes of heating time) and turn off automatically. A great energy saver—especially in these times. Wattages of these ceiling-mounted heaters, range from 660 watts up to 1,515. Some are even made to operate on 240-volt systems.

A TV Set is Another Appliance

You will be pleasantly surprised at the many repairs you can do yourself

Someone in the family always twiddling the knobs? Block them off with conspicuous strips of tape. These controls should be set once and then left as they are.

Markings on the side of your set all refer to the picture tube condition: BRIT; brightness; CONT, contrast; HOR: horizontal hold; VERT: vertical hold. Channel selector controls on top.

WHAT'S A TELEVISION set got to do with electrical appliance repairs? Simple: a TV set *is* another electrical appliance; more complicated than most others, but much easier to handle physically than a clothes washer or an air conditioner.

Repairing a seemingly "defective" TV is much simpler than you might expect, for the simple reason that many of the usual troubles aren't very technical. In fact, much of what is considered "repair" is better described as "maintenance" and is well within the capabilities of most home owners.

Some of the experiences of TV technicians would be funny if they didn't involve the expense of house calls for the customers. Consider the following actual case histories from the records of an electronic service man, and learn from them.

Set Dead. This is a common complaint, but would you believe that in about 50 per cent of all cases the line cord is merely *out of the wall outlet?* The set might have been moved to permit cleaning the floor, and the plug merely pulled away from the wall.

Often a person using a vacuum cleaner removes the TV cord deliberately so that he or she can plug in the vac and then forgets to replace the TV plug. A neighbor might have dropped in for a chat or the telephone might have rung, so the oversight is a natural one.

Weak, Snowy Picture. This could mean a dead tube or transistor in the set, but many times the antenna connections are the fault.

The flat ribbon commonly used for TV hook-ups contains thin wires that break easily when twisted or flexed. If only one of the two leads is separated from the antenna screws on the back of a set, the sound might continue normally but the picture almost always is poor. If both leads separate, both sound and picture usually disappear. Inspect the set and apply a screwdriver to those terminals.

Generally Weak Picture. As a picture tube ages it is bound to grow dimmer, but at such a gradual rate that you don't realize what's happening until a visitor remarks, "How can you tolerate this reception? I can't even tell which team has the ball."

Before you resign yourself to the cost of a new tube and its installation, try something silly, like cleaning the glass face of the set. You might be astonished at the improvement.

Jiggly Picture. this is often due to improper adjustment of two controls that are in open view on the face or the side of the cabinet. If the picture stutters vertically, like a movie film with stripped socket holes, look for a knob marked V, VERT, V HOLD or VERT H. These all mean "vertical hold." Turn the control slowly one way or the other and observe the effect. If the circuitry is intact, you can slow the roll, bring it to a stop, and then start it in the other direction. Return the knob to the steady position and caution other members of the family not to play with it. Better yet, put a strip of tape across it as a reminder.

A warped picture might require adjustment

1—As set ages, it might be necessary to make slight readjustments on the HEIGHT and V. LIN (vertical linearity) controls. These are reached with a small screwdriver through the holes in the back of the cabinet. 2—The antenna connection, right, is often a weak spot. Make sure the ends of the lead-in ribbon are clean and tight under the binding posts. 3—The shafts of the knobs are hollow, and usually are fitted with little flat springs to grip the solid shafts. Note now the channel selector shaft turns inside the fine-tuning shaft. 4—Back of set, lower center, small white objects are vertical and horizontal hold controls.

of the horizontal hold control, marked H, HOR, H HOLD or HOR HOLD.

Don't be afraid to twist these knobs. You can't harm the set, and you might do it a lot of good.

No Picture, Sound Okay. On many sets the volume control and line switch is close to other knobs marked BR or BRIT and CON or CONT. The first abbreviations mean "brightness" and the second "contrast." When a watcher decides to turn off his set, he might fumble for a moment with the knobs before finding the off switch. If he inadvertently turns down the brightness control he effectively turns off the entire picture. The next morning, the woman of the house looks for her favorite soap opera and finds the opposite of a silent movie: sound but no sight.

Bad Color. New owners of color TV invariably go through a hectic period of experimentation with the various controls marked HUE, TINT, COLOR, AUTO/AFT, etc., in an effort to make all color images come through clean and clear. Unfortunately, not all programs are transmitted in such perfect condition. It is not even unusual for two cameras shooting the same scene to give noticeably different color rendition. This is certainly not the fault of the receiver, so it is pointless to call a service technician every time the pictures are not to one's liking. Many color sets are sold with unlimited service contracts, so such calls are numerous.

Old color movies are likely to be especially disappointing because the films have simply faded with age.

The recommended tuning procedure for color TV is to set the controls for the best results from any of the top-rated, nationally-televised shows and *to leave them that way for all future reception.*

INSIDE THE CHASSIS

If you feel adventurous one day you might try opening your set. This is a straightforward screwdriver job, no more difficult than changing the spark plugs of a car and much more interesting. Clean off the top of your workbench, spread an old towel or blanket on it to protect the cabinet, and look it over for the heads of screws or bolts.

Details of construction differ from make to make, but with most sets the back splits from the front after the rear screws are removed. You will notice something here right away: The line cord is connected to a molded jack attached to the inside of the back, and this pulls away from a mating plug on the back apron of the chassis. This is a universally used safety feature, designed to discourage non-technical owners from electrocuting themselves.

If the set has been used for a year or more the chassis will certainly be coated with dust. This is attracted out of the air by the circuitry of the picture tube, which operates on 15,000 to 25,000 volts. Clean out as much as possible with a soft paint brush or a mild blast from a hair dryer with the heating element off.

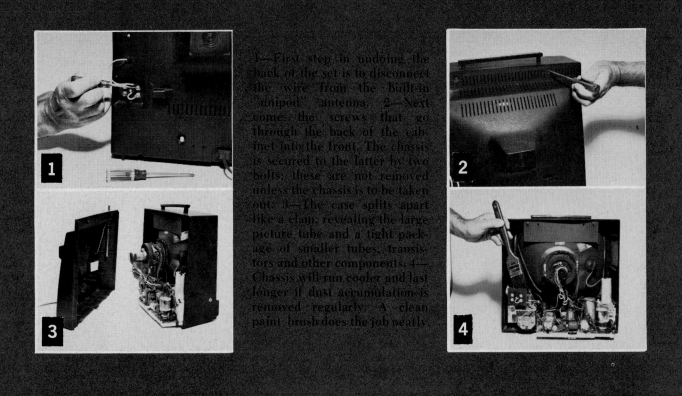

1—First step in undoing the back of the set is to disconnect the wire from the built-in "unipod" antenna. 2—Next come the screws that go through the back of the cabinet into the front. The chassis is secured to the latter by two bolts; these are not removed unless the chassis is to be taken out. 3—The case splits apart like a clam, revealing the large picture tube and a tight package of smaller tubes, transistors and other components. 4—Chassis will run cooler and last longer if dust accumulation is removed regularly. A clean paint brush does the job neatly.

THE TUBES

If the set contains tubes, and if you can reach them without disturbing adjacent components, loosen them one at a time by pulling straight up (*don't twist!*), and immediately push them back down. This movement re-establishes good contact between the pins of the tubes and their sockets, and sometimes improves the performance of the set.

If you're curious about the rest of the receiver, remove the screws that go through the bottom of the cabinet into the chassis. However, before the latter can be freed you will probably have to remove all knobs on the front and possibly on one side of the cabinet. You won't find any setscrews; the knobs are held only by friction springs, you merely pull them off. Take particular note of the design of the channel selector. This usually consists of two separate knobs and shafts. The knobs cannot be interchanged because their shaft holes are of different diameters.

In small TV sets the picture tube is usually mounted to the inside of the cabinet, and the chassis slides out separately. In larger sets the tube is usually mounted over the chassis by means of a saddle-like frame, and the whole works comes out as a single unit. The tube is made of glass, so treat it as you would any glass object. Actually, the glass envelope is heavy and strong, but take care anyway.

In some sets the protective glass on the front panel, covering the face of the picture tube, is held in a frame that snaps out for cleaning. Examine the panel of your set closely, and if there is any sign of an opening around the frame try to pry it off gently with a knife.

ONE AERIAL FOR SEVERAL RECEIVERS

With black-and-white TV sets selling for $100 or less, it is not at all unusual to find two, three or more of them in a household, the exact number depending on the number of children —and the quarrels to avoid. In the strong-signal areas, near TV stations, the sets can be just plugged into wall outlets, as they work satisfactorily with their "rabbit ear" aerials. However, a problem arises in more distant suburban communities: Must the outside of the house be plastered with individual aerials for all the receivers?

No. In most cases a single aerial, elevated as high as the roof construction permits, can serve several receivers with the aid of easily-installed devices called "couplers." These are in effect small transformers that direct parts of the TV signals from the aerial to several sets. The basic unit is a two-set coupler. This has three pairs of screw connectors. The lead-in from the outdoor antenna* goes to one pair; extra lines run from

Footnote:
* The terms "aerial" and "antenna" are used interchangeably.

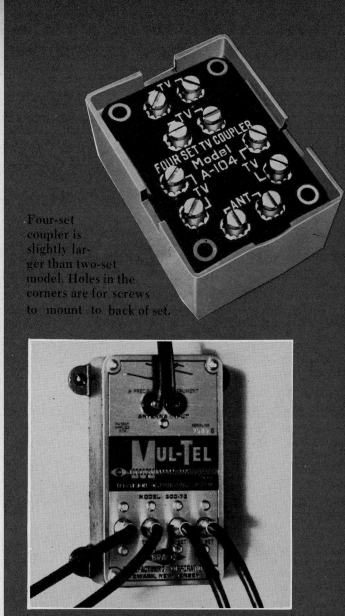

Connections to the two-set coupler are easily made with a screwdriver. It is not necessary to trim wires; the serrated washers cut through.

Four-set coupler is slightly larger than two-set model. Holes in the corners are for screws to mount to back of set.

Shown here is another style of four-set coupler. This model has connections for use by other TV sets or FM stereo equipment needing antennas. The lines are co-axial to deliver a full signal.

the others to the individual receivers. The coupler can be mounted inconspicuously under a window or on the back of a set. If the sets are on different floors it is usually convenient to place the coupler on the upper level and to run the extension line on the outside to the next window below.

The capacity of most conventional antennas is three or four receivers, fed through a four-set coupler. However, depending on the location of a house in relation to the closest TV transmitters, an unpowered coupler might not be satisfactory for four sets; a four-set booster might be needed. As its name indicates, this is a combination of an amplifier and a distribution transformer. It is generally about the size of a cigarette carton, of solid-state design and draws so little juice from the AC line that it can be left on all the time. It requires no tuning or other manual adjustment, and can be installed in less time than it takes to read this description.

In areas where black-and-white reception is good, color reception may be poor because color sets usually require somewhat stronger signals. Because it supplies just the kind of amplification needed for color pictures, a four-set booster can be a very wise investment. If all the sets in a household are color models, a booster is virtually a necessity.

All couplers and booster offer an important bonus: They accommodate high-fidelity FM receivers as well as TV.

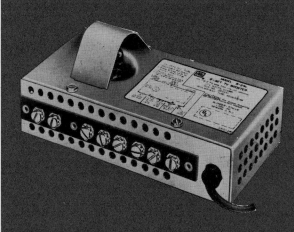

The four-set booster show above is valuable addition to your antenna system if you are in an area where the TV signal is generally weak. This will amplify signals and improve the reception.

The favorite dishes of many lands are made quickly in this Amana Radarange, a table-top model that plugs into a wall outlet. Thickness of door is good guard against possible radiation during operation.

Cooking With Radio Waves

Microwave ovens save hours of cooking time. They also consume far less electricity than the conventional range.

MICROWAVE COOKING

THE INVENTION of microwave cooking resulted from radar research in the laboratories of the Raytheon Corp., during World War II. In 1946, an engineer testing a radar generator reasoned that since its high-frequency energy produced heat in its immediate vicinity it might also cook food. He sent for some popcorn, placed it in front of the radar tube, and was not really surprised when it began popping almost immediately. Experiments with many kinds of foods in dishes of various compositions quickly followed, and from these it was learned that only one-fourth the time required for conventional cooking was needed for the same results with the clean, flameless microwave method.

COST?

By the 1950's Raytheon had developed the first commercially-produced oven, called the *Radarange*. It worked, but because it was large and cost more than $3,000 it was sold mostly to hospitals and other institutions that depended on mass feeding.

Amana Refrigeration, Inc., which became a Raytheon subsidiary in 1965, introduced the first counter-top domestic model *Radarange* in 1967. Selling for $495, it stimulated interest in

and acceptance of microwave cooking by the general public. Other firms were licensed under the Raytheon patents, and today you can buy a 120-volt kitchen model for as little as $349.

HOW IT WORKS

The heart of these ovens is a special vacuum tube called the "magnetron," which generates radio waves at the frequency of 2450 megahertz. These have some of the properties of light waves. They are reflected off metal surfaces; however, they pass right through glass, paper and many plastics. There is no direct heat in the waves themselves; they produce heat in certain materials by agitating the electrons in them. The frictional effect is similar to that caused by the passage of ordinary AC or DC through wires, except that this rubbing occurs at the incredibly high rate of 2,450,000,000 times per second! Among the susceptible materials are most foods, probably because they contain some natural moisture and are therefore slightly conductive. Also included is human flesh, and thereby hangs an obvious headache.

In a microwave oven the radio waves are scattered all around the inside of the cooking chamber by means of a small motor-driven stirrer, which is nothing more than a three-bladed fan, so as to penetrate pieces of food as uni-

84

This Radarange of the 1950s paved the way for the smaller, sleeker models for home use. This chef is displaying a juicy steak that was prepared in one-third the time required for conventional broiling.

Hospitals are great users of microwave ovens, meals can be prepared literally in minutes instead of hours—as these pretty nurses will attest— leaving more time for attention to bed-ridden patients.

Nope, it is not a television set. It is a new Tappan microwave oven. The dial at the right is a time switch, not a channel selector. An indicator lights up when the oven is on; turns off automatically.

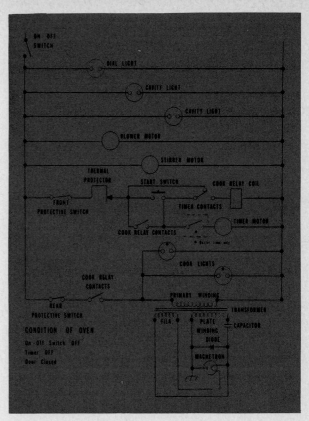

The internal circuit of a typical microwave oven is surprising simple. The transformer at the lower right supplies the high voltage required. Opening the front, or the back of cabinet, turns off current.

formly as possible. Just how well the waves are confined depends on the tightness of the front door, and this in turn depends on the physical design and construction of the enclosure and the degree of quality control at the factory. You wouldn't think this should be much of a problem in this day and age, but do you remember how many bugs you found in the last new car you bought? Poorly assembled ovens of early production leaked like sieves; properly made new ones keep the microwaves inside where they belong.

SAFETY PRECAUTIONS

Just how dangerous any of this radiation is to people has been a matter of controversy for years. Some medical scientists say it is more theoretical than tangible, but eye doctors pretty generally agree that you should avoid looking into an oven directly. What saves the situation for the quarter of a million or so purchasers of ovens is the fact that the outside radiation, when there is any, dies off very rapidly at very short distances from the box.

Installing a through-the-window air conditioner can be done by the average handyman—or woman. You can even even tackle a through-the-wall installation using special sleeve supplied by maker.

Keep Your Cool

A screwdriver, an oilcan, and a vacuum cleaner are all you need to take care of air conditioners.

AS IS THE CASE with refrigerators, there is very little you can do to a window-type air-conditioner except to keep it clean and to make sure that the plug makes firm contact with the wall outlet. It is easier for a home owner to maintain a central air-conditioning system than a window unit, because it usually consists of two separate sections: the heat exchanger, generally mounted on a concrete slab outside the house, and the blower, located in the garage, the attic, or a special closet. In these locations the equipment is usually quite accessible for inspection, cleaning and lubrication. The covers are secured with self-tapping screws and are easily removed and replaced. Open all fuses and circuit breakers feeding the system before you tackle the machines themselves. With straight cooling systems there is generally one double fuse or one double-pole breaker protecting both sides of a three-wire service. In systems that combine cooling with electrical heating there is sure to be an extra fuse or breaker for the heat coils mounted in the air ducts. In systems that combine cooling with gas- or oil-fired heating facilities the latter have their own

two-wire service. Just play it safe and you'll keep your cool.

CENTRAL AIR CONDITIONING

Of the two sections of a central A/C installation, the heat exchanger is the more complicated. One part of it looks exactly like the front end of an automobile; it has a cored radiator and a big fan mounted close to it. Operated by a motor, this fan either blows air through the radiator from the inside or sucks it through it from the outside, the effect is the same. The other major element is the compressor, also motor-operated. This looks like a big iron kettle, completely sealed up. There is little you can do to this except wonder what goes on inside. However, that "little" is important, because it can mean the difference between a dead system and a live one; it is represented by an inconspicuous little button on the case marked Overload Reset, which means just what it says. Very often, pushing this button turns the compressor on again after an inexplicable failure.

The control elements of the system are also in the heat exchanger case, usually in a separate compartment shielded from the radiator fan.

The first step in any electrical job is to turn off the current. If you don't know which circuit breaker controls the appliance you will be working on, turn off the main switch near meter.

In a typical central air conditioning system, the blower may be mounted at the rear of an attached garage. Remove the cover and you will find inside a blower which you should oil twice a year.

CLEANING

Clean out any twigs, insects, grass, paper, etc., that may have drifted in. Use a soft paint brush or air from a reversed vacuum cleaner. Here you might also find a bonus in the form of an instruction sheet or diagram, pasted to the inside of the compartment cover, that contains maintenance suggestions. For example, with the machine shown in the accompanying series of pictures was a note that read, "Annually, lubricate fan motor with not more than 32 drops (about 1/4 teaspoonful) of light machine oil in each bearing." This job took just about 32 seconds.

The blower that circulates air through the house is a barrel-like turbine driven by a husky motor; this too needs periodic oiling. The blower compartment should be kept clean by vacuuming. Any appreciable amount of dust means that the filter in the air return duct is loose in its frame and allows unfiltered air to by-pass it.

Because the cooling-heating system is usually the costliest equipment in a house, pester the manufacturer to send you all available information about it. When you write to the name and address that you'll find on a name plate somewhere on the machine, include the model and serial numbers.

The control system of an air conditioning system is a maze of wires, thermostats, and relays, installed in a separate compartment of the heat exchanger case. Use a vac to blow out the dust.

The return air duct is usually located on a kitchen or hallway door. First remove the grill, then lift out the filter. Handle it carefully and remove the trapped dust with a vacuum cleaner.

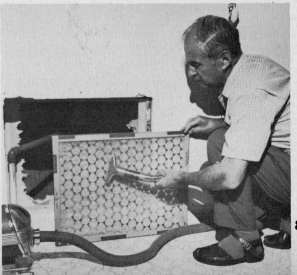

This fine piecer of furniture is easily mistaken for a record player or a portable bar, but it really is a room air cleaner. A break-away view of its construction is shown at right, next page.

Cleaning the Air You Breathe

With forced-air heating systems you can add an electronic air filter or humidifier. But with hot water or steam you must use portable units.

A COMMON PROBLEM in homes having conventional heating systems is excessive dehydration during the winter months. As warm air circulates through rooms it accelerates moisture evaporation, often leaving them so dry that your nose becomes itchy, you get static shocks from metal objects as you walk across carpets, you feel chilly despite high thermostat settings;

books and magazines become brittle, and dust seems to collect everywhere.

THE HUMIDIFIER

Pans of water on radiators and wet towels hung in front of air ducts sometimes ease the situation, but hardly add to the appearance of the house. If you live in a cold northern state and need to keep your furnace running much of the time, you should consider the purchase of a "comfort" machine that is becoming more and more popular—a power humidifier. In its basic form, this consists of a tank of water through which an absorbent belt or wheel rotates slowly as a small fan blows room air through it. Of course, this moist air also evaporates eventually but since it is replenished at a steady rate it alleviates the desert-like discomfort of the heated rooms.

Features of a typical humidifier are an automatic humidistat, automatic shut-off and refill indicator light, variable speed motor, rustproof water reservoir, portability, and an attractive appearance.

A relatively simple plug-in appliance, a hu-

Nope, it is not a hi-fi speaker, but a humidifer, mounted on wheels for easy transportation to any part of the house that requires a bit more moisture during dry, winter months. Construction at right.

midifier is easy to maintain. The motor needs occasional oiling and the wet elements an occasional cleaning. When the heating season is over, the machine can be wheeled into the basement or garage for storage.

THE AIR CLEANER

A second machine that makes indoor life safer and more comfortable is the electronic air cleaner. Remember from your high-school physics days how you could pick up bits of paper with the end of a plastic rod that had been rubbed briskly on a piece of cloth? In a modern air cleaner this same kind of electro-static attraction is provided by a filter of metal plates *not touching each other*, to which a source of about 5,000 volts of direct current is connected. A small fan draws room air over this filter, and the powerful electric charge on it traps up to about 90 per cent of all airborne pollution particles. Mechanical mesh filters take out about 5 to 10 per cent.

Don't be alarmed by that figure of 5,000 volts. The power unit is very small and its energy consumption is small because the electrostatic filter is in effect an open circuit.

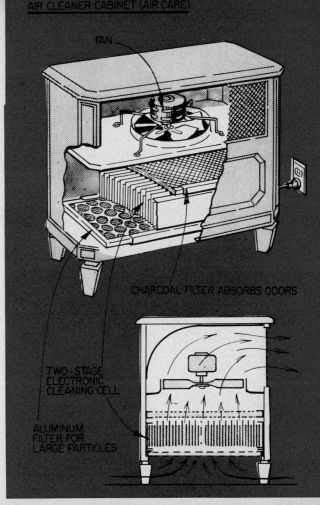

AIR CLEANER CABINET (AIR CARE)

FAN

CHARCOAL FILTER ABSORBS ODORS

TWO-STAGE ELECTRONIC CLEANING CELL

ALUMINUM FILTER FOR LARGE PARTICLES

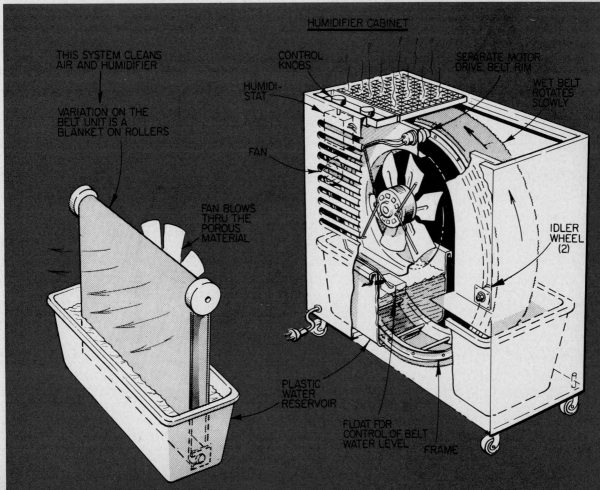

THIS SYSTEM CLEANS AIR AND HUMIDIFIER

VARIATION ON THE BELT UNIT IS A BLANKET ON ROLLERS

FAN BLOWS THRU THE POROUS MATERIAL

PLASTIC WATER RESERVOIR

HUMIDIFIER CABINET

CONTROL KNOBS

HUMIDI-STAT

FAN

SEPARATE MOTOR DRIVE BELT RIM

WET BELT ROTATES SLOWLY

IDLER WHEEL (2)

FLOAT FOR CONTROL OF BELT WATER LEVEL

FRAME

Electric Heating

The cleanest fuel you can use to heat your home is electricity —and the most expensive—but, it can be worth the cost.

YOU OWN a typical six-room, two-story house heated by either steam or hot-water radiators connected to an oil-fired furnace, and you live in an area that gets snow and freezing winter weather. You are getting a bit tired of the dirty job of removing black soot from the boiler and of maintaining, repairing or replacing oil and water pumps. You read somewhere that electric heat is flameless and therefore clean. Furthermore, it doesn't require a big tank that occupies valuable space in the base-

ment and it works promptly and silently at the flip of a switch. Undeniably, these are attractive features, so you begin to think about the possibility of taking advantage of them.

You might as well stop thinking right now, because there is no way of substituting an electric heater element for the roaring flame of an oil burner. If you want to get rid of the latter in order to reduce maintenance work, your best bet is a gas conversion unit—providing of course that the house has piped-in gas. If you

Compactness and simplicity are features of electric furnaces as this view of a partially opened Amana shows. Heating elements are in upper section of cabinet. Drum-type blower is at bottom of cabinet.

cook with bottled gas or electricity, you're stuck with the oil guzzler.

The gas conversion unit is merely an enlarged version of the burners on a kitchen range. It installs easily and quickly, and requires only a new pipe to the existing line now running up to the kitchen. The present thermostat is retained. A safety device on the furnace closes the gas valve if the pilot light goes out because the gas supply is interrupted. This is a simple but highly reliable arrangement, universally used with gas heat.

IS IT PRACTICAL?

Electric heat is practical if three requirements are met: electricity is cheap, very cheap; the house has a duct system for forced warm-air circulation; you are prepared to sell the present flame-type furnace for junk and to replace it by an entirely new machine of the all-electric variety. Adapting the latter to the ducts is a simple mechanical job.

It might be possible in some cases to install heavy-duty electric strip heaters in the duct leading out of the furnace, and to continue to use the blower alone with the oil or gas line closed off.

Two persons should be consulted to determine if either a new or a converted electric system should be considered seriously. One is a representative of the local utility and the other is an electrical contractor with experience in this work. Since a power company makes money only by selling electricity, it welcomes a heavy user, but only if the electric service in the vicinity of the house can handle an increased load. Let's face it: electric heat takes a lot of current, sometimes twice as much as all the electrical appliances in a house combined.

Kilowatt-hour rates for electricity vary enormously from one section of the country to another, depending on the type and cost of the fuel that run the turbines that turn the genera-

A combination heating and air-conditioning unit is of course larger than furnace alone. The distribution ducts fit over the opening at the upper left of cabinet. Sizes range from 5 to 25 kilowatts.

tors. The current itself is not the only element of cost. To it must be added the price of a special transformer and a separate cable to the house from a high-voltage distribution circuit that might be several blocks distant.

If you have a good house with a duct system you can do a really worthwhile renovation by installing a single unit that provides both winter heat and summer cool, as the outside temperature changes. The ducts are a permanent part of the house, so you might as well take advantage of them. A central "comfort system" will certainly pay for itself several times over if you decide to sell the house at some future time.

In the southern and southwestern states, where winters are short and mild, and summers are long and hot, the majority of new homes are built with central systems as described. The emphasis here is on the air conditioning capability. The electric heaters in the ductwork need only moderate amperage, as their job is merely to take the nip out of January and February mornings. Therefore, their cost of operation is nominal, and their load does not strain the power cables.

When some central heating systems are inadequate and cannot be enlarged economically, or if you have a vacation home than requires only a spot of heat on occassion, a separate electric baseboard or wall heater with its own thermostat may be the best way to solve the problem. Drawing below shows one version

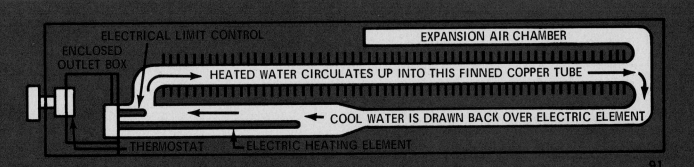

ELECTRICAL LIMIT CONTROL

ENCLOSED OUTLET BOX

EXPANSION AIR CHAMBER

HEATED WATER CIRCULATES UP INTO THIS FINNED COPPER TUBE

COOL WATER IS DRAWN BACK OVER ELECTRIC ELEMENT

THERMOSTAT   ELECTRIC HEATING ELEMENT

Gardening is a real pleasure if your entire garden is in this movable cart, both levels are illuminated by incandescent and fluorescent lamps. Note the timer at the right, set for 14 hours of light in each 24-hour period.

Gardening Indoors?

No need to confine all your gardening to the outdoors. Choose the right lights and you can have your green thumb throughout the year.

HAVE YOU SWORN OFF GARDENING because you got tired of fighting the vagaries of weather? If you still like plants and flowers and would love to have them brighten up your home, why not grow them right *in* your home instead of outdoors? Using artificial light from ordinary incandescent and fluorescent lamps, you can turn your basement or any other available space into a colorful garden that thrives all year round no matter what the weather is outside.

An electrified greenhouse differs from a conventional greenhouse as the latter depends on daylight and sunlight, which are not dependable at all. Indoors, *you* adjust the light to the right color and for the right exposure, at your convenience.

TIMING THE LIGHT

Light is a critical source of energy for plants. Their appetite for it varies. Some thrive on sunshine or its equivalent; others grow best in shady spots. The rhythm of alternating periods of daylight and darkness is also a factor in their development. For the hobbyist with a little electrical know-how, all this means is using a clock-timer to turn the indoor lights on and off.

Of course, plants need more than light; all normal horticultural practices must be followed. These deal with soil composition, watering, fertilization, etc.

GROW THESE PLANTS

Probably the most popular plant among hobbyists is the African Violet. This requires little bench space, responds gratifyingly to controlled light conditions, and is really beautiful to behold. Other plants that thrive indoors are Anthurium, Baby Tears, Cactus, Calla Lilly, Hyacinth, Phlox, Snapdragons, Tulips and Genista.

COLOR RESPONSE

Plants respond to light of varying color. White light is a mixture of all colors, and the "white" light emitted by an incandescent lamp is rich in red while the "white" light of many fluorescent lamps is rich in blue. In general, red light causes plants to become tall and "leggy." Blue light when used alone can cause low, stocky growth. A proper balance of red and blue energy produces plants that have normal growth and shape.

In research growth chambers of the United States Department of Agriculture and others in horticulture departments of several universities, it has been established that a mixture of fluorescent (rich in blue) and incandescent (rich in red) lighting gives better growth results than those produced by either alone. Combined lighting is accomplished by supplying about 10 per cent of the light intensity with incandescent lamps. This is a ratio of about two fluorescent watts to one incandescent lamp watt.

Many flowering plants, favored by hobbyists, are known to grow well with fluorescent lamps as the sole source of light. However, plants grown under incandescent lamps alone are inclined to be spindly and pale in color.

FLUORESCENT FIXTURES

Standard industrial and commercial fluorescent fixtures are widely used by the hobbyist. Special fixtures for plant-growth applications provide for combining fluorescent and incandescent lamps.

Where higher lighting intensities are needed, the use of individual channels, each holding one fluorescent tube, is inexpensive, and permits arranging lamps in closely spaced banks for high light levels.

LAMP REPLACEMENT

All lamps darken with age, and the resulting loss of light eventually becomes appreciable. Old or blackened lamps should be replaced so that plants do not suffer from lack of light. At 70 per cent of life (about the 525-hour point) incandescent lamps provide about 15 per cent less light than when new. The output from most fluorescent lamps is similarly reduced at 70 per cent of life (about 8,500 hours).

For long-term optimum performance, lamps should be given regular attention, including washing or dusting the reflectors and lamps regularly. Wall surfaces, as in a basement where plants are grown, should be painted white for maximum reflection.

A less elaborate type of an indoor garden. A pair of fluorescent lamps is housed under the top of the stand. Have your husband build this simple stand— and you will never have to garden in the rain.

This home-built basement garden produces a lush crop of seedlings under the bright lights of a dozen 8-ft.-long fluorescent lamps. Winter-grown seedlings are the transplanted outdoors in spring.

Prize-winning plants grown by a gardening enthusiast who has 7 lighted carts like this in her basement. Timers control a 14-hour "day". Another advantage of indoor gardening is freedom from bugs.

93

Electric Motors

You probably have ten or twenty electric motors of various types in your home. Most will run for a lifetime without care if they are not abused.

Because of the nature of its job—collecting dirt and dust—a vacuum cleaner should be inspected frequently and its brushes checked for wear and length. First step is to remove the outer bell.

After removing the end bell on this Electrolux, a second protective plate comes into view and motor can be seen through it. Remove nuts that hold plate; use pliers only if wrench is not available.

The end of the motor that carries the commutator and the brushes will now be exposed after removing the plate. Use a brush, or a second vac as a blower, to remove the fluff. Clean all areas thoroughly.

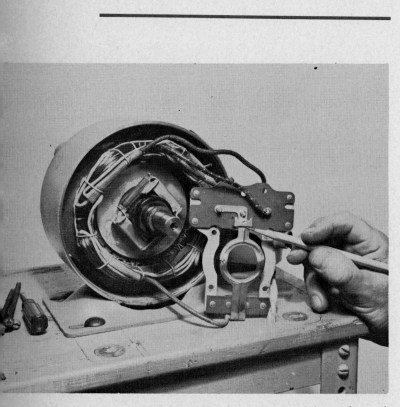

The switch plate has been removed from the end bell. Pencil points to the switch that controls the starting winding. Contacts are closed when the motor is started and open up after it is running.

ELECTRIC MOTORS

THE ELECTRIC LIGHT banished darkness, and the electric motor banished household drudgery. How could any modern woman get along without such labor-saving appliances as the vacuum cleaner, dish washer, clothes washer, dryer, mangle, hair teaser, can opener, juicer, blender, disposal . . . all of them motor operat-

ed? Without motors there would be no refrigerators, freezers, air conditioners, oil burners or water pumps. And where would the automobile be without its electric starter?

It is fortunate that electric motors as a class give long and faithful service, and require only simple maintenance such as cleaning and oiling. Perhaps once in its lifetime, the type known as "universal" might need new brushes. These are little bars of ordinary carbon about an inch long and between ¼ and 3/8 inch square in cross section. Mounted on one end of the motor frame in insulated, spring-loaded holders, they press against the terminals of coils of wire wound on the rotating member of the motor. These terminals take the form of thin copper strips on an insulated sleeve, called the "commutator," on one end of the shaft.

The rotor winding is connected in simple series with another winding on the inside of the motor body, called the "stator."

This motor is often called an "AC-DC" because it runs equally well on both kinds of current. The term is really obsolete because there is no longer any commercial 120-volt DC service in the United States.

The term "universal" is more appropriate because the motor is used in a large variety of appliances ranging in size from hand-held grinders to vacuum cleaners on wheels. It starts readily and attains high speeds, which can be controlled easily by the same plug-in solid-state devices used as dimmers for incandescent lamps. This speed control is self-contained in many new models of portable hand drills, saber

saws and similar tools; in hair-drying machines; and in blenders, mixers, and other food-processing appliances.

It is easy to distinguish a universal motor from other types because the brush holders are always mounted diametrically opposite each other near one end of the shaft. They are usually in open sight, for easy inspection and cleaning. In some vacuum cleaners they are inside an end "bell" of the case to protect them from the dirt pulled in by the machine.

There is another way to identify the universal. The faint sparking between the stationary brushes and the speeding commutator often creates electronic interference. In a radio set this takes the form of a high-pitched whine; in a television set, white spots dancing across the screen. It can be eliminated by connecting a small capacitor across the brushes.

Lubricate a universal motor very sparingly. Oil is a good insulator, and if even a drop of it splashes away from a bearing to the commutator the motor will run erratically until the friction of the brushes against the commutator dries it away. Many motors intended for intermittent running don't have oil holes at all. Some have one, at the end of the shaft without the commutator.

Model trains use a simplified version of the universal motor. This retains the rotor winding, the commutator and the brushes, as described, but instead of a wire-wound stator it has a powerful little Alnico magnet of the same shape that does the same job. It runs on low-voltage DC from the combination of a step-down trans-

This is the commutator end of the motor. The copper bars that are embedded in it are separated and insulated from each other. Each bar is connected to one of the coils of wire on the motor's rotor.

In this particular machine, the end caps of the brush assemblies are secured by screws. When the screws are removed, the brushes pop out under the pressure of the coil springs attached to the ends.

These are the parts of a shaded-pole motor—it has no brushes or commutator. Motor frame with stator windings is in center.

Carbon from the brushes which lodges on the commutator can be removed by rubbing with fine sandpaper, finish with a cloth.

In small machines, such as this jig saw, brush holders are conveniently located on outside of the case. Pencil points to brush.

In this capacity start split phase motor diagram, Lr is the running winding, C the fixed capacity, S the centrifugal switch.

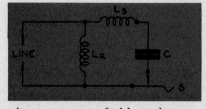

former and a solid-state rectifier connected to the AC line. Very conveniently, a locomotive containing a motor of this kind can be made to run equally well backward or forward by means of a simple reversing switch in the DC leads to the brushes.

THE SHADED POLE MOTOR

A second widely-used type of motor is the "shaded pole." It has a wire-wound stator, and a rotor, but the latter does not have an actual winding or a commutator. Instead, it usually consists of a cylindrical iron core with a series of thin copper bars imbedded in it lengthwise. The AC from the line creates a varying magnetic field around the stator. This field induces a current in the nearby bars, and the current in

turn creates another magnetic field in the iron core. The first field acts on the second field, just as two small magnets attract or repel each other. The net result is that the whole rotor assembly spins in step with changes of the line current. The shaded-pole motor is more properly called the "induction" type, because of the interaction of the magnetic fields.

Without commutator and brushes, the shaded-pole motor is cheap and easy to manufacture and is virtually foolproof in operation. These virtues have a price: It has relatively low torque (i.e., turning force) and does not start readily under a heavy load. However, it is en-

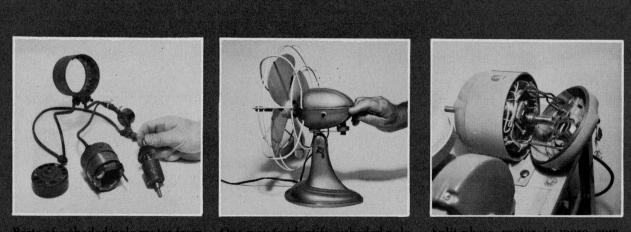

Parts of a shaded pole motor from a fan. It ran fitfully. Taken apart, it showed the cause. Bits of lint between stator and rotor.

One way to identify a shaded pole motor is by looking at the case; it will usually have no brush-holders visible, as in this fan.

Split-phase motor is more complicated. When end bell is removed, starting and running coils are visible for examination.

tirely satisfactory for steady, predictable loads such as imposed by fan blades, timing mechanisms, etc.

THE SPLIT-PHASE MOTOR

Most of the motors for relatively heavier duty in household machines such as coolers and washers, and in shop machines such as saws and drills, are induction types also, but with the important difference of superior starting. This is achieved by the use of two stator coils, one called the starting winding and the other the running winding. When such a motor is at rest, the two windings are connected in simple shunt, so when the line switch is snapped on current flows to both of them. Acting together, they exert a strong magnetic twist on the rotor and jerk it into motion. The motor picks up speed, and after a second or two a centrifugal switch on the shaft opens and cuts the starting winding out of the AC circuit. This type of motor is called "split phase." The opening click of the switch as the machine starts, and the closing click as it coasts to a stop, can often be heard quite clearly.

In some split-phase models the centrifugal switch is replaced by an external time-delay starting relay, which serves the same purpose. This unit is generally small enough to fit in the base of a motor-operated machine such as a bench grinder.

Even better starting ability is provided by a split-phase arrangement that includes a capacitor in series with the starting winding. As this component is three to four inches long and up to about two inches in diameter, it is usually mounted on the outside of the motor case. Its hump-like shape is unmistakable.

Because motor repair is very expensive, when available at all, overload protection is very important. With loads so great that they simply stall the shaft (a common occurrence with clothes washers that are stuffed too full), the circuit breaker or fuse in the AC line opens before any real damage is done. In the case of a washing machine the cure is to lighten the load by removing a few garments at a time until the breaker or fuse holds fast. One make of washer has a built-in scale for weighing the clothes and carries a strongly worded warning not to exceed the prescribed limit.

Even with normal loads, motors that run for long periods in confined spaces with poor ventilation are bound to heat up. Some models are made with built-in thermal circuit breakers for protection against actual failure. These are of two types, the automatic reset and the manual reset. The first is entirely within the motor frame. When the machine gets too hot, the AC goes off, and it doesn't come on again until the motor has cooled down to a safe level. If the process repeats itself more than a couple of times the whole installation needs investigation. Sometimes, just blowing dirt out of the motor with a vacuum cleaner clears the trouble. The automatic feature cannot be bypassed, so the protection is positive.

The manual reset protector can be spotted quickly because of its little red head sticking out of the motor case. This pops when the motor overheats and cannot be pushed back until the temperature drops. *Don't force it!* If it appears to be stuck, it is stuck, purposely.

Pencil points to weighted arms of governor. As motor attains full speed they open a switch removing starting load from the AC line.

This typical drill press motor has its starting capacitor mounted piggy-back fashion on the frame of its 1/3 hp., 120-volt motor.

An easy way to keep an electric motor clean is to blast it with a vacuum cleaner. Connect the hose to the exhaust side to blow.

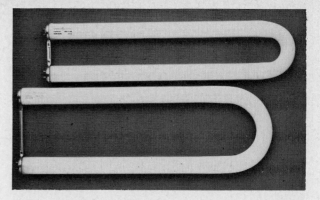

New U-shaped fluorescents are spaced 3½ and 6 inches between the arms. A box, 24 inches square, can accomodate two or three lamps. This triple unit provides a soft light over desk or workbench.

Ideas for Indoor

A lamp for reading in bed should be about 22 inches from the book. A double bed, or a pair of twin beds, can be illuminated with one or two 48-inch fluorescent lamps installed in a plywood box.

THE MOST COMMONLY USED electrical device in the home is also the simplest, the cheapest, the most versatile and the most beneficial to all members of a family. It is the electric light, probably the greatest contribution to humanity by the greatest electrical inventor of the past 100 years, Thomas A. Edison.

Actually, the basic concept of the electric light originated with other experimenters of the mid-19th Century, but Edison did something with it that all the others failed to do; *he made it work*. And it continues to work, to proliferate in types, styles and sizes. There are at least 500 different bulbs on the market, and new ones appear regularly. A recent innovation is the bent fluorescent illustrated.

Electric light is no longer just a means of illumination. It is an important factor in interior decoration, and contributes to the appearance of a home and to the comfort of those who live in it. At low levels of brightness furniture and drapes tend to look dull and lifeless. As the illumination is increased, they become alive and vibrant. In a dark room people tend to be quiet and morose. In a brightly lighted one they are likely to be talkative and outgoing.

The residential lighting specialists of the lamp division of Westinghouse and General Electric have many ideas of interest to home owners. A few of them are shown on the following pages.

Lighting

New bulbs and fixtures combined with dimmers can make your lighting more glamorous and functional. Here are some tested ideas.

Two recessed fixtures at the left and how they are used in the home for living room illumination and den lighting. These fixtures are sold prewired, ready for connection after cutting a suitable opening.

The valances around this room hide fluorescent light tubes to provide soft, even, lighting. Construction details for ceiling-mounted and wall-mounted installations are shown in sketch.

This kitchen has a 150-watt ceiling fixture for general lighting and 40-watt fluorescent units under the cabinets to light the work area. The 150-watt table fixture can be raised, lowered.

Ceiling fixtures can be incandescent or fluorescent, either recessed or surface mounted. Fluorescents have an advantage because they produce three times the light of incandescent lamps

Four lighting units dreamed up by the lighting experts of GE. This combination desk and bookcase is 7 ft. high and is made of ½ and ¾-in. plywood; it is 34 in. wide, 12 in deep. Alter size to fit room.

The sewing center has the light overhead to provide soft, even lighting. The light colored background prevents possible eye strain when sewing. Cabinet at right serves as a handy accessories storage bin.

Incandescents, because of their compactness, offer a multitude of lighting applications. Living room wall at right has recessed spots to illuminate paintings. Below: A—Pole lamp with three adjustable reflectors, to direct light around room and on work area. B—Wall-mounted shade fixture can be raised or lowered. C—Adjustable spot in ceiling.

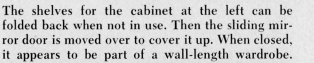

The shelves for the cabinet at the left can be folded back when not in use. Then the sliding mirror door is moved over to cover it up. When closed, it appears to be part of a wall-length wardrobe.

Note shadowless lighting on the lucky girl who has this vanity. Lighting is achieved by means of 14 incandescents of 25 watts and two overhead warm-white fluorescent tubes, covered by a valance.

Dramatic Lighting

Dimmer switches and hi-low toggle switches make it possible to vary the intensity of your lights to fit the mood.

UNTIL RECENTLY, the only way you could control the illumination in a room was to vary the *number* of lights that were on or off; the individual bulbs could not be dimmed. This changed with the development of easily-installed "dimmers" that work as simply and smoothly as the volume controls on radio and TV sets.

In most dimmers made for home use an on-off switch is combined with the actual brightness control. In some, the AC to the lamp is off when the knob is turned counter-clockwise (to the left) until it clicks. It is on when the knob is twisted slightly the other way. In other models, the switch is push operated. With either type, turning the knob gives any degree of brightness from full to a scarcely noticeable red glow and then to nothing.

With this flexibility, all sorts of dramatic and useful effects are possible. For example:

In a dining room, soft light to resemble that of candles, with none of the latters' fire danger. A slightly bright level if the tablecloth is dark, or a lower level if it white. Or full brightness if the affair is informal, the guests dressed casually, and the overall atmosphere cheerful.

For TV viewing, only enough room illumination to enable you to find your way in and out without stumbling over furniture.

For all-night light in a baby's room, a hallway, a bathroom, etc. Similarly for security purposes, half-bright lights on a porch, over a garage and in a basement, etc.

Real professional effects for amateur theatricals.

Dramatic lighting of works of art such as paintings, sculptures, photographs. Try bright spotlights on these, with all other room lights turned about half-way down.

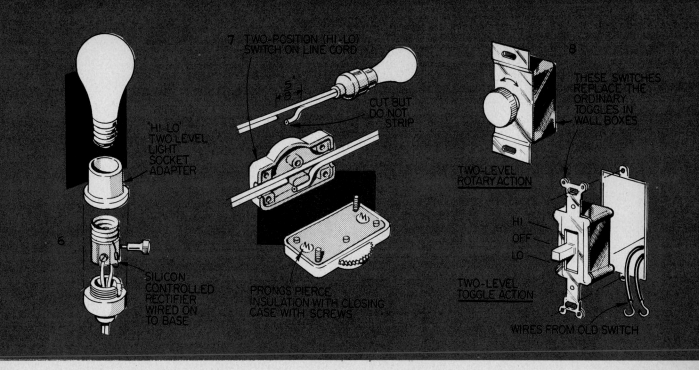

Various types of dimmers are shown in the accompanying illustrations. The most popular model by far is the one that replaces any standard on-off toggle switch in a wall box. The only tool you need for the job is a screwdriver. After removing the fuse or opening the breaker on the circuit, you can make the replacement in a few minutes.

The wattage capacity of dimmers is marked somewhere on their bodies. The wall type mentioned is usually rated at 600 watts, the equivalent of six 100-watt bulbs. Most rooms don't have more than half that much light.

It is important at this point to mention that the dimmers obtainable in hardware and electrical stores are almost without exception suitable only for incandescent bulbs, the ordinary screw-in type. Fluorescent lamps are not nearly so adaptable. In fact, conversion is not really practical with *existing* fixtures because it requires a different "ballast" (the transformer-like part inside the body of the reflector), as well as rewiring. However, full flexibility of control is available in newer styles of fluorescents specifically designed for dimming.

In many homes a wall switch controls only the ceiling lights or a single wall outlet. For control of individual lamps, the simplest plan is to wire a small dimmer into the line cord; this does not involve a change of any kind in the lamp itself. You can buy dimmer-adapters and replacement sockets with the dimmer built-in, as well as a handy portable remote-control model that requires no work at all; it just plugs in.

Table-top dimmers have a capacity of up to 300 watts. Plug it into an outlet and then plug the lamp into the dimmer. More than one lamp can be used if they do not exceed the total wattage.

Resting at your elbow, with a quick twist of the wrist you can adjust this table-top dimmer switch to produce the desired light. Dimmers that replace lamp sockets are also available.

The lighting fixture in this breakfast nook has a 600-watt dimmer switch in the adjacent wall. Some chandeliers have a cluster of incandescent bulbs that exceed this wattage so check accordingly.

The small dimmers for insertion into lamp cord are usually rated at 200 watts and have a rotary-action switch. It might feel slightly warm to the touch, this is normal.

For some purposes continuous adjustment of illumination is not needed. For example, a simple high-low control is often adequate for a basement or bathroom light. Dimmers of this type look exactly like switches and have three settings: off, high and low.

Perhaps you have the notion that house-lamp dimmers are like the dashboard dimmers of cars. In purpose, yes; in construction no. The latter are rheostats. These are variable resistors which reduce the lights by wasting some of the battery current to them in the form of heat. AC dimmers use tricky new solid-state devices called "thyristors." In effect, these are rectifiers that keep some of the AC back, without wasting it, so a bulb doesn't shine as brightly as it would with all of the current.

Speed controls, which are incorporated in

Lighting in this basement playroom is incandescent and perimeter flourescent. The three 75-watt separate "high hat" fixtures are controlled by a switch with three positions: high, low and off.

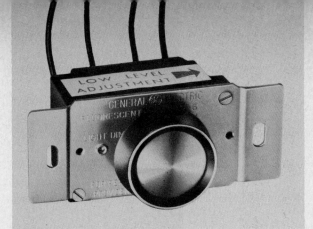

Fluorescent dimmer switches occupy the same space as incandescent dimmers but can only be used with fluorescent fixtures that have special circuits. Fluorescent dimmers have four leads.

many hand power tools such as drills and saber saws, are similar to light dimmers. However, they work only with small fractional horsepower motors of the series type, which can be recognized by the presence of two carbon brushes that make sparking contact with a rotating spool-line section of the shaft, the commutator.

One of the less-recognized features of dimmers is the great increase in the life of bulbs that they make possible. Also, since they burn at lower temperatures than normal for considerable periods, inside blackening of the glass is reduced.

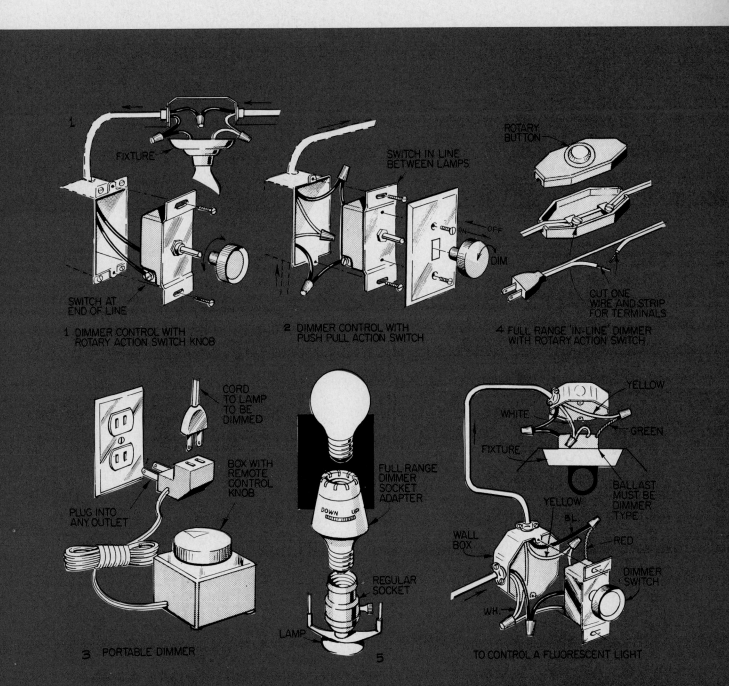

FIXTURE

SWITCH AT
END OF LINE

1 DIMMER CONTROL WITH
ROTARY ACTION SWITCH KNOB

SWITCH IN LINE
BETWEEN LAMPS

ON   OFF

DIM

2 DIMMER CONTROL WITH
PUSH PULL ACTION SWITCH

ROTARY
BUTTON

CUT ONE
WIRE AND STRIP
FOR TERMINALS

4 FULL RANGE IN-LINE DIMMER
WITH ROTARY ACTION SWITCH

CORD
TO LAMP
TO BE
DIMMED

BOX WITH
REMOTE
CONTROL
KNOB

PLUG INTO
ANY OUTLET

3   PORTABLE DIMMER

FULL RANGE
DIMMER
SOCKET
ADAPTER

DOWN   UP

REGULAR
SOCKET

LAMP

5

YELLOW

WHITE

GREEN

FIXTURE

BALLAST
MUST BE
DIMMER
TYPE

YELLOW

WALL
BOX

BL.

RED

DIMMER
SWITCH

WH.

TO CONTROL A FLUORESCENT LIGHT

Dips after dark can be enjoyed with greater safety when a pool is illuminated. Low voltage fixtures are recessed into the side walls of this pool. Additional lighting at bases of trees, at the grouping of chairs and the pool ladder area contribute to safety and beauty.

Landscape Lighting

Lighting up your entranceway or back yard is usually for security and safety. But it also can be beautiful. Here are some ideas.

EXCITING NEW DIMENSIONS can be added to family living by lighting the areas surrounding the home to enhance their intrinsic charm, beauty and utility at night. Extending imaginative patterns of indoor illumination to outdoor areas—gardens, patios, pools, work and play spots—is not only consistent with good, overall home planning but opens up whole new vistas for more family enjoyment and safety.

Well-planned residential outdoor lighting creates a total home environment combining maximum esthetic appeal with efficiency. It makes the home and its surrounding grounds complementary and endows the entire living area with a distinctive aura of unity and completeness in all seasons. When light is brought outdoors, it reveals the beauty of gardens, trees and foliage. It expands the hospitality and comfort of patios and porches and stretches the hours for outdoor recreation or work.

The accompanying text and illustrations show how to capture the mystery and subtle qualities of night lighting—how to light ground contours and focal points—how to create silhouetted forms and shadow patterns—how to use colored light—and many other ways to make any home more attractive, safer and just plain fun to live—through imaginative outdoor lighting.

MODELING

Depth and three-dimensional character can be given to exterior objects at night by lighting them from several directions. A large tree, for example, can be modeled by casting light upon it from one or more directions, thereby emphasizing various aspects of its form. More light from one side than the other accentuates the effect. A smaller tree can be lighted from two sides with a spotlight from one side and a floodlight 90° away. The space or distance between the light source and what is to be lighted is extremely important in determining both the area that it lights and the light level. Light from a distance is often much more effective but is not always possible. Light sources placed too close to objects of medium to high reflectivity can create excessive brightness which spoils the effect.

HIGHLIGHTING

Highlighting usually refers to special lighting for patios and other outdoor living areas or for small flower beds that require lighting emphasis. Lighting equipment can be mounted high in trees and aimed down to light a garden

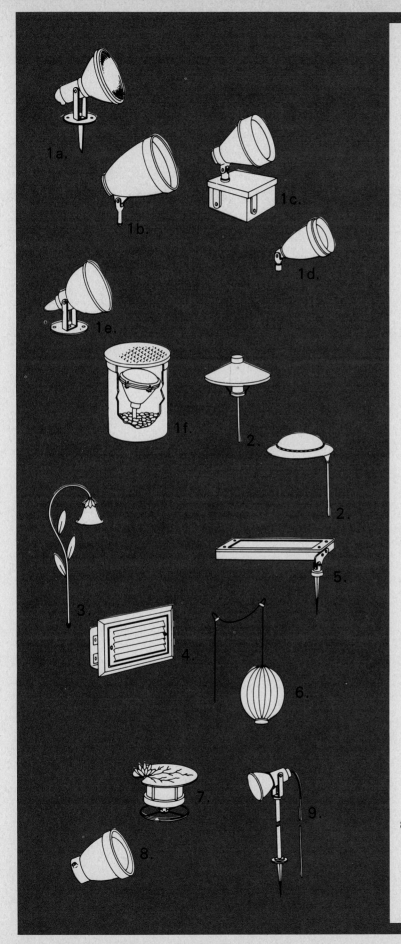

1. **Adjustable Holders** — for PAR 38 projector lamps and others with spike for ground placement, cover plates for outlet boxes and attachment clamps for use on tree or pole. USES — for all areas described in this publication.

a. for PAR lamps. Color glass covers, louver and shield clip on bulb.

b. of metal, offers deep shielding, better appearance.

c. mercury floodlights — adjustable units mounted on enclosed ballast.

d. for R20 floodlights. Cover lens protects bulb.

e. enclosed floodlights — often called "handy floodlights". Use up to 300 watts. Cover glass protects regular household and reflector bulbs.

f. flush mounted fixtures for projector lamps. Specific housings available for 150PAR38 up to 500PAR64 and for mercury lamps. USE — in open areas without available natural shielding.

2. **Mushroom Unit** — use with any height stem or post. Both side-suspended and center stem type available. Wide range of reflector width, depth and contour result in differences in complete bulb shielding. USES: general lighting on terrace with 4 to 5 foot stems; most visual tasks with 100 watt bulb, placed at rear corner of chair; circulation areas; flowers and plants of all heights. Bulb wattage: as desired. (Many variations of the basic mushroom design are available).

3. **Bell-type Reflector** — Suspended from fixed height stem with lamp base up. USES: flowers and plants in small area. Garden steps.

4. **Recessed units** with lens or louver control. Directs light down about 45° below horizontal. Bulb wattage: from 6 to 25 watts depending on unit. Locate from 4" to 24" above ground. USES: Paths and walks near buildings — 8 to 12 feet apart; steps — mounted in risers or adjacent building; terraces to light floor — 6 to 10 feet apart.

5. **Weatherproof fluorescent units** — wattage depends on length of unit. USES: where line of light is desired.

6. **Diffusing plastic shade** attached to suspended socket. Various sizes, shapes. USES: general lighting for terraces with roof or overhang — 40 to 75 watts in 10" diameter units — 100 to 150 watts in larger sizes. Decorative: with 10 to 40 watt colored or white bulbs.

7. **Underwater fixtures** — lily pad shield attached to glass enclosed housing. Use 25 to 60 watt bulb.

8. **Underwater fixtures** — provide controlled light. Bulb size depends on unit. Available in both low voltage and 120 volts, depending on unit.

9. **Telescopic poles** for PAR38 and enclosed floodlights. Fit into pipe sleeves driven into ground. USES: sports and area floodlighting.

An outdoor outlet is a great convenience in the garden. It should always be the 3-wire grounding type. Make provisions for several outlets when planning lighting system.

area, or mushroom-type fixtures can be spiked in the ground to emphasize certain parts of a garden. Highlighting can also be accomplished by lighting the viewing side only. Attention can be directed to low plantings by placing low-wattage lamps in front of them. A similar effect can be achieved by concealing strings of Christmas lamps in a small trench in front of the plantings.

SHADOW PATTERNS

Shadows can be used to create broken or solid patterns and to introduce the excitement of movement from tree branches or foliage. The object which casts the shadow—house, plant, ornament or other—doesn't have to be visible. The elongated shadow of a group of poplars or

LIGHT BULB COLORS	RELATIVE LIGHT OUTPUT	WHAT THEY WILL DO
White	100%	Good on reds, oranges, yellows. Will gray blues.
Blue-White	40% Sky Blue 39%°	Emphasizes reds, pinks, greens, flesh tones.
Pink	75% Dawn Pink 52%°	Excellent on red foliage—flattering to people but not to green foliage.
Green	17%°	Will exaggerate greens but kill reds and pinks.
Blue	5%°	Will exaggerate blue tones.
Yellow Amber	77%° 57%°	Good on yellow, orange, brown foilage.
Red	7%°	Will exaggerate red tones.

°(100-watt PAR lamp)

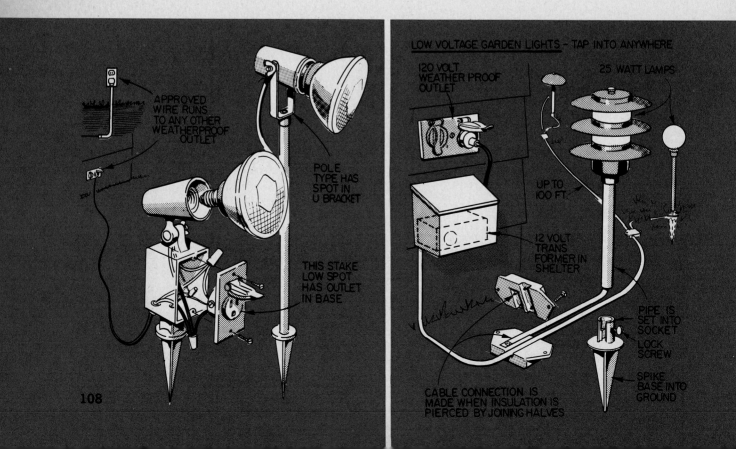

a row of hollyhocks, for example, can convey the suggestion of another area, with imagination creating the remainder of a visual impression for the viewer. Spotlights create more clearly defined patterns than do floodlights. If either a spot or floodlight is placed very close to the object, a fuzzy shadow pattern will result. This may not be desirable when lighting a single object, but a shadow pattern cast by a solid mass is best if it is fuzzy rather than well defined.

SILHOUETTING

Exterior objects having interesting line and form are frequently best lighted so they are seen in silhouette, either as a dark object against a lighted background or a luminous material against darkness. The first method is to light wall, fence or shrubbery *behind* the object with very little light on the front. Silhouetting objects against darkness is achieved by shining light through translucent materials such as certain types of leaves and other foliage.

GRAZING LIGHT

Grazing light can be used to great advantage in emphasizing the textural qualities of tree bark, hedges, masonry, fences and many other outdoor objects. Light sources should be aimed parallel to the surface of objects (four to ten inches out from the surface) since "head on" lighting flattens the appearance of the material and minimizes the desired lighting effect.

TINTED LIGHT

Tinted light is used primarily for emphasis —to bring out the color in flowers, shrubbery and special objects. Generally, light of the same color as the object to be lighted, is a good choice for heightening its color. White flowers, highly-saturated colored flowers or gardens with mixed colors look most natural under white light. Low-wattage incandescent lamps, being yellower in tone, tend to deaden the color of grass and foliage. Better foliage color results from using lamps of higher wattage, cool white or daylight fluorescent tubes or with sky blue bulbs.

All colored fluorescent lamps have saturated colors and will cause distortion of the actual colors in nature. Fascinating treatment can be given to objects by mixing red, blue and green light—the objects are seen in white light but surrounding shadows are seen with tints of color.

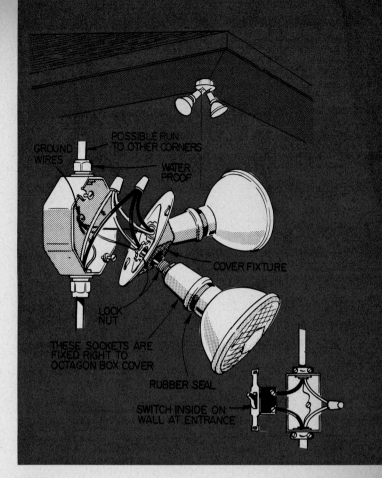

WIRING

Outdoor lighting equipment can be installed on building structures or anywhere in the yard and garden. Equipment and wiring may either be permanently installed or temporary. All equipment and wiring should be weatherproof. Permanent wiring usually should be run underground. Underground wiring can be enclosed in metal pipe or Type UF cable may be used. Sand or light gravel around the wire will help water drainage, and a board over the wire will protect it from picks and shovels. UF cable must be at least 18 inches below the ground when it is buried directly. Conduit or wire can be run to various areas of the garden to convenience outlets or to permanently installed equipment.

All portable cords and outlets, if used, should be grounded. Most portable lighting equipment is supplied with six-foot or longer watherproof cords. Additional portable cord is available in various lengths. You can get cords designed specifically for outdoor use with suitably molded rubber plugs and sockets. Some lighting equipment also has built-in outlets into which additional units may be connected.

LAMPS

The most useful bulb types are the following:

Wrap a protective ring of sponge rubber or tire inner tube around the trunk before tightening stainless steel clamps that hold fixture in place. Always use outdoor 3-wire extension cords.

1. **A-line.** A typical household bulb can be used out of doors mainly in mushroom-type equipment, path-light equipment, lanterns and wall-mounted brackets. The 15- and 25-watt lamps can be used without protection from water. Higher wattages need shielding from weather.

2. **Reflector lamps.** Popular, self-contained spot and flood-lamps, these light sources need protection from weather, too. Available in the following: 30, 50, 75, and 150-watt sizes. Higher

wattages are available but are not normally used in landscape lighting. The 75- and 150-watt reflector lamps are available in both spot and flood-light distribution. The 30 and 50-watt lamps are available only in a medium flood distribution.

3. **PAR lamps.** Molded out of heavy heat-resistant glass, PAR lamps are rugged. They are unaffected by rain or snow but must be installed in fixtures having a weather-tight seal at the socket. The 75 watt PAR and the 150 watt PAR are available in both the spot and floodlight distribution. Higher wattages are available for longer throws and where a well-controlled high intensity beam of light is needed.

4. **Quartzline lamps,** available in wattages from 250 watts to 1500 watts, can be used for general lighting such as sports areas. Their advantages are high efficiency, long life, excellent lumen maintenance and good lighting control in fixtures specifically designed for them.

5. **Colored lamps.** A wide array of colors are available in A-line bulbs, PAR and reflector lamps. A-line or ordinary household bulbs come in Dawn Pink in 40, 60, 75, 100, and 150 watts and Sky Blue in 60, 75, 100, and 150 watts. Seven colors are available in the 75-and 150-watt reflector lamps and in the 100-watt PAR lamp. Two of the colors are tints, the pink and blue-white. Two colors, the yellow and the amber, are of medium intensity. The red, blue, and green are strong colors which are normally recommended for holiday decorating or unusual specialty effects.

6. **Fluorescent lamps.** Fluorescent lamps can be used in weatherproof fixtures where lines of light are desired. Equipment is available in sizes ranging from 15 watts to 40 watts. For outdoor lighting, use cool white, daylight, blue or deep blue.

7. **Sign lamps.** Transparent incandescent sign lamps are available in white and eight colors. The colors are saturated and therefore are recommended only for decorative party-type lighting outdoors. They are weatherproof.

8. **Christmas strings.** The outdoor-type Christmas bulbs can be used for outdoor lighting without protection. Normally, the clear and white lamps are the only ones used for garden lighting but color bulbs can be used for a party effect. Twinkle lights would be annoying and are restricted in their use.

9. **Low-voltage lamps.** There is a growing demand for low-voltage lamps for outdoor lighting. The most commonly used low-voltage lamp

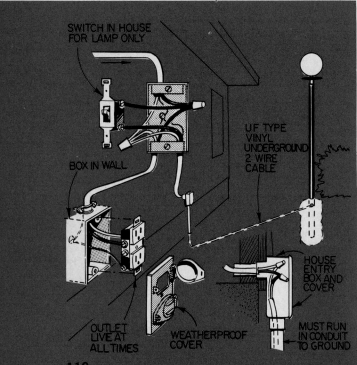

SWITCH IN HOUSE FOR LAMP ONLY

BOX IN WALL

UF TYPE VINYL UNDERGROUND 2 WIRE CABLE

OUTLET LIVE AT ALL TIMES

WEATHERPROOF COVER

HOUSE ENTRY BOX AND COVER

MUST RUN IN CONDUIT TO GROUND

is the 12-volt lamp. The 25-watt and 50-watt lamps come in three beam shapes, narrow spot, wide flood and very wide flood.

OUTDOOR LIGHTING EQUIPMENT

A wide range of outdoor lighting equipment is readily available. Many factors related to mechanical design as well as electrical features are important but lighting effects desired are primary considerations in equipment selection. Both day and nighttime appearance of fixtures should be carefully checked. And be sure bulbs and wiring are concealed from direct view.

Weather resistance cannot be overlooked since lighting equipment is subjected to sun, rain, wind, snow and sand. Aluminum, brass, copper, stainless steel and even plastic are used in fixtures today.

Durability is a prime concern in picking outdoor lighting equipment and the cost of fixtures is usually directly proportional to durability. Equipment must be able to stand up under a great amount of abuse throughout the year—not only against weather but also the destructiveness of lawn mowers, snow throwers, dogs, children—even adults.

Check to see if equipment is easy to re-lamp when required. Also, ask about any possible problems in installation. Note the accessories such as the base, ground spike, pipe and

Power to this outlet is supplied by a 3-wire cable (the third wire is for grounding) protected by steel conduit. Caution: never use BX cable for any outdoor work—dangerous and illegal.

cord length and type, electrical convenience outlets, others. Any special wiring instructions?

Fixture design and color normally should blend in with the landscape and should be as inconspicuous as possible, day or night. Most garden lighting equipment is finished in black or green or matte aluminum. Green blends with most types of foliage and is a very practical color when shielded by garden plantings. Black or dark green equipment mounted adjacent to a tree trunk is inconspicuous in most cases.

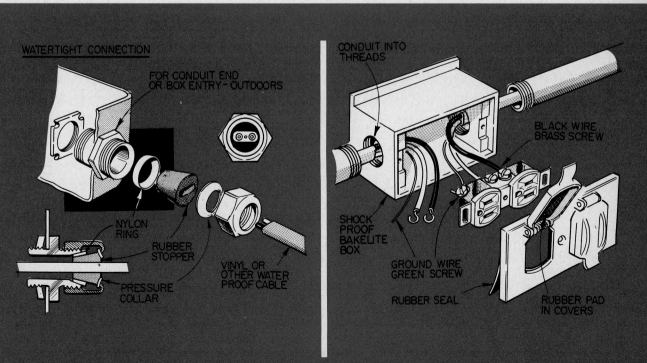

Lighting For Security

The increased rate of home burglaries triggered the growth

AROUND ENTRANCE-WAYS, paths and walks, steps, garages and recreational areas of private homes and apartments, lighting installed for convenience and accident prevention provides additional benefits by deterring prowlers and vandals.

An interesting aspect of protective lighting systems is that intruders rarely seem challenged to outwit them. Perhaps it is the passive quality of light which quells the spirit of malicious aggression, or perhaps the rationale is more simply put: where there is light, someone cares, someone is likely to be watching. Law enforcement officials have frequently pointed out that lighting on properties surrounding occupied buildings creates points of visual interest giving occupants a reason to look out. Thus they become watchers, and thus are feared by the intruder.

In the scheme of community affairs, lighting is not only beneficial as a deterrent to aggression, but also has value in that a deterred

crime incurs no cost for police action, no cost for prosecution. So the crime-deterrent capability of lighting has economic value and ample justification for community-wide "Light the Night" campaigns.

Following are some typical recommendations and brief comments about several universal factors that apply for selecting and using lighting equipment in typical residential areas.

ENTRANCEWAYS

Light Sources—Incandescent lamps from 25-watt decorative types to 150-watt PAR lamps are widely used sources.

Types of Equipment—Usually preferred are wall-mounted brackets in pairs, one on each side of the door. Effective mounting location is 5½ feet above standing level. A single fixture, at the same height, is best located on the lock side of the door; or is also effective centered above the door. Good alternatives also are re-

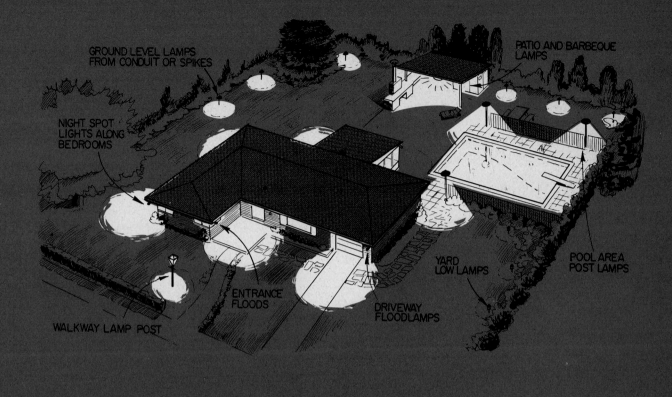

Labels on illustration:

GROUND LEVEL LAMPS
FROM CONDUIT OR SPIKES

PATIO AND BARBEQUE
LAMPS

NIGHT SPOT
LIGHTS ALONG
BEDROOMS

YARD
LOW LAMPS

POOL AREA
POST LAMPS

ENTRANCE
FLOODS

DRIVEWAY
FLOODLAMPS

WALKWAY LAMP POST

An excellent example of a well lighted driveway, entrance walk and front door area. The garage, lamp post and door light are all connected to the same switch. Build a timer into the circuit.

and Safety

of the alarm systems. But exterior lighting is still the best way to deter crime.

cessed units in the ceiling or roof overhang. Those fixtures mounted higher above the standing level require higher-wattage lamps; at least 60-watt lamps for side brackets and 75-or 100-watt lamps in above-the-door fixtures.

The luminous *quality* of fixtures is a factor often overlooked. They can be architecturally compatible for daytime viewing but offensively bright and glaring at night; shielding the light source is essential. Frosted or opal diffusing glasses are preferred: clear glass is tolerable only when low-wattage lamps are used and the ambient light level is fairly high.

In ceilings of external entranceway structures or in roof overhangs, recessed or surface-mounted units can be installed. Although overhead units in most cases are out of the direct line of sight on approach, they require light source shielding with some sort of diffusing material; their brightness can be annoying. Recessed fixtures, often unobtrusive, give high levels of light for the horizontal surfaces under-

foot as well as in the vertical plane, that is, on callers' faces.

The best location for a single fixture is centered close to the entrance door. Larger areas can, of course, be covered with multiple fixtures. Square fixtures are usually equipped with one 100-watt lamp, whereas some rectangular types with two lamp sockets offer better end results. In either case, shielding with diffusing material is necessary. Installations that incorporate both decorative wall-mounted fixtures and recessed functional lighting equipment often work best. The visible fixture's brightness and styling are for appearance, and the recessed equipment principally for the light level necessary for seeing and safety.

STEPS, PATHS AND WALKS

Light Sources—Applicable generally are 25-watt to 150-watt incandescent lamps, and Deluxe White mercury lamps in the 50-watt to

175-watt range. The mercury lamps are more efficient, and they have longer life to sustain safety and protection for greatly prolonged periods between burnouts.

Types of Equipment—There are several types of equipment for mounting below eye level, to light ground areas: ground-spike units and units with louver or lens plate light distribution control for installation in walls adjacent to paths or walks. Overhead units are available for tree or pole mountings. And there are post-top and wall-mounting lanterns designed for both decorative style and functional lighting.

Ground-lighting units installed below eye level normally light, at best, no more than an eight-foot diameter area, coverage being influenced by the size and shape of the reflector. Complete shielding of below-eye-level light sources is obviously necessary. When used alongside stairs, particular attention should be given to shielding because of possible low viewing angles. Spacings are generally considered effective if the semi-dark interspaces between pools of light are not greater than the breadth of the light pools. Louvered or lens plate type equipment designed for installation in walls adjoining paths are effective if mounted 16 and 24 inches above ground and not more than eight feet apart; they are also effective if recessed in stair risers.

Post lanterns are effective lighting tools provided their design has not rendered them glaringly bright or restrictive in light distribution toward ground levels. Frosted glass diffusion, at least, is usually adequate; heavier diffusion materials are better. Prismatic lens control is best. It is excellent as a light distribution feature. A light distributing reflector built in above the lamp adds to effectiveness, depending on the type of reflector. For wall-mounting units that serve functions similar to post lanterns, the same features apply.

The post lantern is excellent solution to the distribution of light on ground areas, and the visible lamp is of low-wattage with agreeable brightness. Another variation has a second lamp in the cap above the glass panels. Equipment of this sort is effective along paths and drives when spaced not more than 25 feet apart.

Overhead floodlighting from poles 10 to 20 feet high offers the advantage of widespread light distribution or sharp spot beam control. Floodlighting lamps are effective in shields nine inches or more deep to hide the visible brightness of lamps. Low-voltage bulbs are another choice; they have built-in shielding that minimizes spill-over of light.

This striking display of plants at the entrance of a house is actually a ground-to-ceiling glass enclosure, accessible from inside the house through louvered door shown at the left of main door.

Two valuable accessories for security lighting systems are the photo-electric and clock-timer controls.

SWIMMING POOLS

Swimming pools and the lounging areas around them represent a potential safety problem because the people who use them are wet much of the time and are therefore fairly good conductors of electricity. The underwater lights

Lamps, recessed into the soffit, brings out the texture of the flagstone wall, and also lights the path to the entrance door. Note the illuminated house number at far right, a real boon to visitors.

The traditional post lantern light is always popular. This one uses a powerful mercury lamp that floods the ground with light. Some post lanterns have a built-in outlet for operating electric tools.

Using standard incandescent lamps in strategically located fixtures, this house becomes an attractive picture each evening. The post lantern takes a 100-watt lamp, other fixtures use 75-watt lamps.

Inviting, is the word for this pool with its background of lighted trees. The underwater illumination is furnished by two 12-volt PAR floodlights for absolute safety to nocturnal swimmers and waders!

that give a pool a glamorous appearance at night were a special headache when they used ordinary 120-volt lamps in water-tight fixtures that weren't water-tight. However, the shock danger for swimmers disappeared when pool builders sensibly switched to 12-volt lamps run by step-down isolation transformers connected to a 120-volt line.

If you want to convince someone that this low voltage is really safe, have him or her touch wet hands to the terminals of an automobile battery.

The GFI

GFI means GROUND FAULT INTERRUPTER.

A device that can save you from dangerous or potentially lethal shock.

LEAKAGE OF ELECTRICITY from appliances to persons using them, with an accidental "ground" forming the return circuit to the power line, has long been a problem. The danger is minimal if all the wires and connections inside the metal case are well insulated from the latter and also from each other, or if the case is made of an insulating material. Potential trouble develops when interior insulation dries out or wears away because of vibration, and bare wires finally touch the frame. If the appliance is fitted with a three-wire line cord, terminating in a three-prong plug that fits into a matching outlet, the first such internal contact (a real "short-circuit") will almost certainly blow out the fuse or circuit breaker on the line. No one can ignore this danger signal.

UNGROUNDED APPLIANCES

However, many of the common appliances found in the home do *not* have three-wire safety fittings: irons, coffee pots, toasters, mixers, can openers, fans, vacuum cleaners, lamps, razors, hair dryers, radio and TV sets, etc. They can continue to run in perfectly normal fashion even if they have the dead internal short-circuit just described, but touch them with the juice on and you'll be lucky to escape with just a dazed expression on your face. If you were leaning against a stove, sink, radiator, or refrigerator, at the time you wouldn't be reading this right now.

What have been described are extreme but by no means infrequent occurences. The internal breakdown in an appliance does not have to be complete; if it is partial, the leakage of current is merely lower. A person doesn't have to be in direct contact with a perfect electrical ground such as household piping to get a shock. A damp floor or wall is in effect also grounded; not very well, but often well enough to complete a circuit.

Some appliances that are absolutely cold electrically when dry can become lethal if water is allowed to seep into them to form a conducting surface between the case and exposed connections inside. Moisture on any electrical de-

The top of a ladder is no place to discover that a drill is giving you a tingle. This portable GFI going up with a construction worker has outlets for four appliances. It is Hubbell's Circuit Guard.

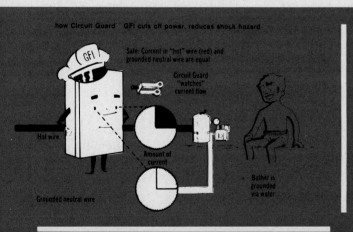

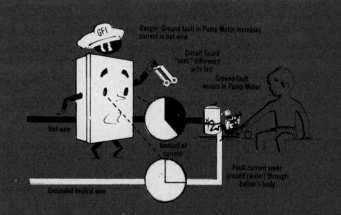

These simplified drawings give a general idea of how a GFI works. The secret is their fast reaction to accidental leakage of current. If as little as 5/1,000th of an amp goes the wrong way,—to the body of a bystander—the internal sensing circuit cuts off the AC in a fraction of a second.

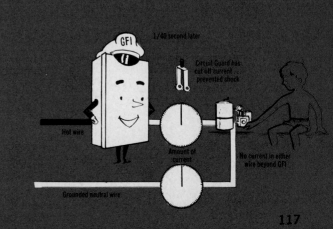

Left: a prime application of a GFI is the protection of users of a swimming pool against possible current leakage from the pump and water purification system. Pump cord is plugged into a GFI.

What woman using a hair dryer wouldn't feel more comfortable knowing she is protected against current leakage, from the motor or the heating coils, by means of this GFI plugged into wall outlet.

These children can swim safely in this school pool because all the electrical circuits around it are first fed through GFI shown mounted on the wall at left; they are mandatory in some communities.

vice is bad. Operating any appliance with wet or damp hands is bad—twice over.

THE GROUND FAULT INTERRUPTER

The three-wire grounding system unquestionably has saved many people from shock. Additional protection is now available in the form of new devices called "ground fault circuit interrupters" or "ground fault interrupters," or in shortened form merely as "GFIs."

These take advantage of the fact that the current in a "ground fault" (the accidental path between an ungrounded wire and ground) represents an extra load on the power line, which passes through the GFI. The difference is very slight, but it is enough to unbalance a sensitive

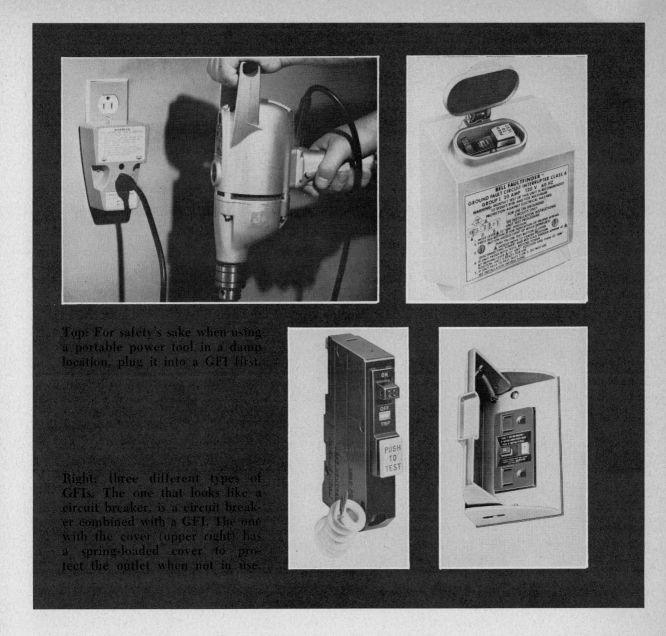

Top: For safety's sake when using a portable power tool in a damp location, plug it into a GFI first.

Right: three different types of GFIs. The one that looks like a circuit breaker, is a circuit breaker combined with a GFI. The one with the cover (upper right) has a spring-loaded cover to protect the outlet when not in use.

solid-state circuit which in turn kicks the AC off.

HOW IT WORKS

The question everyone asks about GFI is, "The short-circuited current has to flow through a person's body to complete the circuit and to trigger the device. Why isn't he shocked just as he would have been without it?"

Let's say right off that a GFI *does not eliminate shock*. However, it triggers when the body current differential is only 5 milliamperes, which is far below the 50 or 60 figure considered to be really dangerous, and it flips the current off in about 1/40th of a second. The actual amount of energy in the shock (the combination of the small current and the short time that it flows) is so limited that a victim feels hardly more than a slight jolt. The important thing is

that he is *able* to feel it—and to *remember* it!

The GFI has already proved its value as a safety measure. However, it is not and cannot be a substitute for careless electrical habits, such as making changes in power circuits with bare hands with the current on or for poor maintenance of appliances and machines.

DIFFERENT TYPES

GFIs take two forms: adapters that plug into wall outlets, for use with one or two appliances, and fixed units combined with circuit breakers for permanent installation in branch panel boxes. They are of particular and special importance in normally wet areas, such as laundry rooms and swimming pools. In fact, the National Electrical Code specifies GFIs for these applications.

119

A flashlight should always be kept on hand for emergency lighting, plus candles. Place lighted candles in jars to avoid drafts.

What To Do Before A Storm

Our tremendous power requirements that cause generator breakdowns, plus electrical and wind storms, can cause power failure. So be prepared!

YOU CAN'T REALLY APPRECIATE how thoroughly electrified our life is until you encounter a "blackout." Not a "brownout," which is only a reduction of voltage, but a 100 per cent loss of power. However, you might be able to minimize the effects of such occurences if you heed some of the suggestions given to its customers by the Florida Power and Light Company. Serving the fastest growing section of the country, an area that also happens to be vulnerable to hurricanes, this utility has had much practical experience with emergencies. Their recommendations are included in this chapter.

PRELIMINARY CHECKLIST

Know in advance where your service entrance equipment is located so that you can check quickly and safely for a blown fuse or tripped circuit breaker.

Keep an adequate supply of fuses accessible; make certain they are of the proper type and size.

Always have a workable flashlight in your home.

A battery-powered radio can be a valuable asset during a power interruption. If you have one, be sure it's in working order.

If for some reason your lights go out, check lights and appliances in other rooms and see if your neighbors have power. If you still have power elsewhere in your house, or if your neighbors' lights are burning, chances are you have blown a fuse or tripped a circuit breaker—

a warning that your wiring is overloaded or a short has occured.

TO REPLACE A FUSE

1, Pull fuse blocks marked Main at service entrance to cut off power while you replace burned fuse; 2, disconnect the lamp or appliance that you believe caused the fuse to blow; 3, be sure your hands are dry, and stand on a dry surface when removing or replacing a fuse; 4, look for the blown fuse. Usually the mica window is blackened or a gap in the element can be seen; 5, when removing or inserting a fuse, grasp just the rim between thumb and forefinger; 6, replace the blown fuse with a new one of proper size; 7, replace Main fuse blocks for restoration of power.

A TRIPPED CIRCUIT BREAKER

Results from the same cause as a blown fuse. Take the same precautionary measures as

IMPORTANT. During any power interruption—regardless of the nature or duration—immediately turn off major electric equipment: air conditioners, washers, dryers, television sets, heavy-duty motors. Otherwise, when the electricity comes back, the sudden surge caused by these load demands could blow fuses in your home; in the event a broad area is affected by the outage, the momentary surge could complicate and delay power restoration efforts.

prescribed for fuses and carefully follow instructions on the panel to reset the circuit breaker.

If your neighbors are without power, there has probably been a minor equipment problem. Call your utility company and steps will be taken immediately to determine the source of trouble and restore your service.

POWER INTERRUPTIONS

Brief interruptions of a more widespread nature may occur for such reasons as: equipment malfunction; damage to facilities caused by falling trees, auto accidents, electrical storms; fires in commercial or residential areas which make it necessary on occasion to shut off power as a safety measure.

Widespread outages are immediately "reported" by automatic monitoring equipment. Therefore, it is not necessary in these instances to report loss of service or to seek progress reports via telephone. A battery-powered radio will keep you informed on power restoration efforts.

If still without power after all service restoration is announced, you should then report the trouble to your utility.

WIDESPREAD POWER INTERRUPTIONS

During severe storms, electric service may be interrupted as the result of damage, or it may be shut off as a safety precaution. In these circumstances, the outages could be widespread and of extended duration.

Inconvenience can be minimized by observing certain precautions as the storm approaches.

CONSERVE REFRIGERATION

Turn your refrigerator and freezer to a colder setting. Open only when absolutely necessary and close quickly. Both will stay cold much longer if these precautions are taken. Well-constructed and insulated home freezers, filled with food, will maintain food-preserving temperatures up to 48 hours.

If you need emergency refrigeration, use regular ice in ordinary refrigerators and in the refrigerator section of your combination refrigerator-freezer. Use dry ice *only* in frozen food cabinets and in the frozen food compartments of combination refrigerator-freezers.

Provide for water. Your water supply may fail. Sterilize your bathtub and other containers by scrubbing thoroughly; then saturate a cloth or sponge with ordinary bleach and swab the container. Let it dry. Then fill with water. Boil water before drinking.

These reserves can also be used to operate toilets by partially filling the tank.

Check emergency cooking facilities. Be sure adequate fuel is on hand. Provide an ample supply of canned foods and milk.

Plan for temporary lighting. Check candles, lamps and flashlight batteries and bulbs.

Use telephone for emergencies only. If damage is widespread, your utility company has systematic plans for complete service restoration. Please call the company only to report any hazardous conditions you might observe, such as live electric wires. Overloaded switchboards may prevent completion of *their* essential calls. Report individual trouble only after service is back on in your neighborhood.

Transitor radios will keep you informed of what's cooking during a blackout. Make sure you have fresh extra batteries always handy.

Black Light

"Black light" is produced by a very unusual type of bulb and lends itself to many applications both in the laboratory and in the home.

THE VERY TERM "black light" sounds like a contradiction, but it isn't. It designates near-ultraviolet radiant energy, that part of the spectrum just beyond the violet light that is visible to the human eye. This ultraviolet is produced by electric lamps that look like ordinary lamps but behave quite differently.

When black light shines on a fluorescent material (that is, a substance that glows when properly excited), an energy conversion takes place. Depending on the chemical nature of the material, the latter absorbs some of the energy and reradiates it as visible light, producing visual effects that are dramatic. There are many kinds of fluorescent paints, lacquers, water colors, inks, dyes, chalks, crayons, pencils, papers, fabrics and powders that lend themselves to endless applications, particularly decorative ones, with very simple equipment.

Black light lamps fall into three categories:

Incandescent, filament type. The General Electric 250-watt *Purple-X* has a special filter-glass bulb that transmits the desired near-ultraviolet energy but absorbs most of the visible light produced by the filament. Because this bulb becomes rather hot, the makers recommend that it be used intermittently, perhaps five minutes on and ten off. Also, it should be used in a heat-resistant porcelain socket, never in the ordinary kind having a cardboard insulating shell. The *Purple-X* is useful for close-up examination of minerals, stamps and similar objects.

Mercury. Most mercury lamps produce both visible and black light, and require external filters to absorb the visible part.

Fluorescent. There are two kinds, designated BL and BLB. The BL differs from standard fluorescents only in the composition of the phosphor, the chemical coating on the inside of the tube. The BLB is like the BL but uses special glass for the tube so that it is its own filter and cuts off the visible light from the phosphor.

Filters are important in black light applications because they eliminate or reduce the visible light and thus make the black light more effective. They are obtainable in various thicknesses, colors and shapes.

A small, low-wattage black light stand made especially for stamp examination is a good investment for a philatelist because it tells him in a second if a stamp has undergone tampering to make it rarer. For example, washed-off cancellation marks show up plainly.

Conventional Christmas tree and other holiday trappings acquire an entirely new appearance if they are painted, sprayed or dipped in fluorescent chemicals and illuminated by black light. With trees, the light fixtures are best placed on the floor so as to shine through the branches. For the home, the most suitable sources are 15- or 20-watt BLB fluorescents in aluminum reflectors; 100-watt PAR-38s 100- or 175-watt R-40s. Of course, for maximum visual effect regular room lights should be turned off.

OPTICAL EFFECTS

The psychedelic effects that are popular with teen-agers for den and playroom background are easy to obtain with various combinations of fluorescent paints and flashing black lights. There is virtually no end to the weird lighting that can be produced.

A more useful application for black light is in insect traps. These are effective in attracting night-flying bugs because their eyes are sensitive to near-ultraviolet and blue. As the unsuspecting insects near the black light they are sucked in by a fan and then either electrocuted by a wire grid or drowned in a water tray. For illumination of the protected area yellow bulbs should be used because this color is not visible to the flying bugs.

Note carefully that the widely used yellow (amber) "bug light" does *not* repel insects; it just does not attract them the way a regular white lamp does.

A good source for black light devices at reasonable prices is Edmund Scientific Co., Barrington, N.J. 08007.

National Electrical Code

As a home owner interested in electrical work, you should be fully familiar with the National Electrical Code and also your local building code.

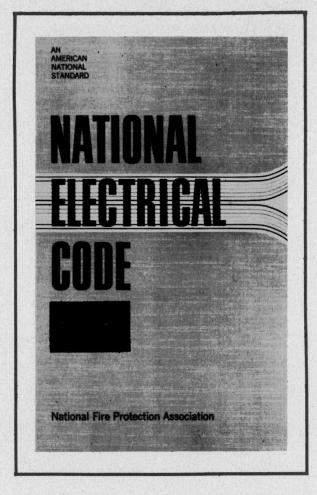

IN MAGAZINE ARTICLES dealing with home wiring there are frequent references to the National Electrical Code (NEC) and its specifications for wiring, safety devices, outlets, switches, and grounding. Many people have the impression that the code is an official promulgation of the federal government and that its word is law. This is not so.

The NEC is actually a publication of the National Fire Protective Association. This is a group of various insurance companies, electrical manufacturers, and architects whose common interests are security and fire prevention. The original code first appeared in 1897 under other auspices, but has been sponsored by the Association since 1911. It is purely advisory, and the Association has no authority or power to force it on anyone. However, because life and property protection are of such obvious importance to home builders and home owners alike, a good deal of the Code is accepted by many commu-

nities and incorporated into their own local building codes.

The latter vary widely and often wildly from one town or county to the next. For example, a town might specify that all joists must be 2x4s, all interior walls of plaster over metal lath, all garages set back not less than 50 feet from the curb line, and all wiring enclosed in thin-wall conduit. Another town, a few miles away, might allow 2x3s, dry walls, garages next to or under the house, and BX (flexible armored cable) wiring. The buyer of a house, even if he is having it custom-built, has no control over these factors. Of course, he can pay the builder to exceed the minimum requirements and thus assure himself of a better house (in his own estimation), but he cannot ask the builder to go below the minimum.

Suppose the builder tries to cut corners. Who checks on him? The sharp-eyed inspectors of the building department of the community. And what can they do if they uncover some non-code work? All they have to do is refuse him a "certificate of occupancy." This leaves him with a house that he cannot turn over to the waiting buyer.

Once a house is completed and occupied, the owner has no obligation to anyone but himself to keep himself and his family alive and under shelter. If he feels like running a 25-foot extension of flimsy lamp cord to carry juice to a 20-ampere air-conditioner, he'll need more than an air-conditioner to cool off the smoldering wire. The NEC is protective, not restrictive.

In small communities there is not enough demand for copies of the local codes to justify printing them in quantity. However, since they are regarded as public information, you can usually see a copy in the city hall or other municipal office. Identify yourself as a property owner and tell the clerk you merely want to keep abreast of the law.

The full National Electrical Code is a fat book of 536 pages. Much of it covers industrial plants, theatres, movie and TV studios, communication systems, etc. This makes interesting reading, but an abridged version entitled "One-and Two-Family Residential Occupancy Electrical Code" is more useful to owners of such homes. For a copy send two dollars to the National Fire Protective Association, 60 Batterymarch St., Boston, Mass., 02110.

INDEX